DISASTERS

By Tom Conklin

SCHOLASTIC
PROFESSIONAL BOOKS

NEW YORK • TORONTO • LONDON • AUCKLAND • SYDNEY
MEXICO CITY • NEW DELHI • HONG KONG

Thanks to John Clissold for help and ideas.

Cover design by Pamela Simmons
Interior design by Solutions by Design, Inc.
Interior illustrations by Ivy Rutzy and Ron Zalme
Photo research by Sarah Longacre
Interior photo and illustrations: pages 9, 10, and 11 by Ron Zalme, pages 25, 26, 27, 60, 64, 76, 78, and 80 by Ivy Rutzky; pages 16, 19, 34, 37, 38, and 39 from North Wind Picture Archives; page 61 © AP/Eric Draper.
Cover photographs: Earthquake © AP/Anat Given;
Volcano © National Geophysical Data Center, Boulder, CO; Hurricane © AP/Victor R. Caivano

ISBN 0-590-98823-9

Copyright © 2000 by Tom Conklin

Table of Contents

The Death of the *Titanic*

PART THREE: NATURAL DISASTERS

Earthquakes: Ready to Rumble

Hurricane!

Introduction

Masters of Disasters

It's true: People are fascinated by disasters. It seems as if you can't turn on the news, pick up a magazine, or visit a movie theater without coming across a story about individuals encountering cataclysmic events.

Children are especially drawn to disastrous stories. Rampaging dinosaurs, doomsday asteroids, tornado chasers, sinking ocean liners: these are the subjects of popular movies geared to young audiences. Why are these terrifying events so compelling?

There are many reasons, but one in particular stands out. By seeing disasters unfold, we understand their causes and consequences. By learning about brave individuals who either survive a disaster or sacrificed themselves so that others might survive, we discover a model of behavior for our own lives. By watching or reading about disasters, we "master" them, and doing so, we master our own lives.

The study of disasters also happens to present marvelous opportunities for classroom instruction. This book has been planned and written to help you explore ancient, man-made, and natural disasters in your classroom. Each chapter focuses on a specific disaster or type of disaster, and presents a variety of activities and reproducible pages to help your students comprehend the causes and consequences of each. The activities span the curriculum and encourage cooperative learning. Each chapter could stand alone as a separate unit of instruction, or could be combined with others to form a more comprehensive disaster unit.

The book is divided into three sections. Part One: Ancient Disasters, looks at disasters from long ago. The book opens, ironically enough, with a "doomsday" disaster by exploring the possible causes for the mass extinction of dinosaurs. The second disaster, The Wrath of Vesuvius, continues with a look at the volcanic eruption that buried Pompeii 2,000 years ago.

Part Two: Man-Made Disasters, presents in-depth explorations of the Johnstown Flood and the wreck of the *Titanic*, two terrifying events in which human arrogance, combined with the cruelty of nature, resulted in terrible loss of life.

Part Three: Natural Disasters, provides hands-on activities that explain earthquakes and hurricanes. The overarching theme of this section is that while nothing can prevent these natural events, people can prepare and be ready when they strike.

This book will use your students' natural fascination with disastrous events as a springboard for instruction on science, math, language arts, and social studies. Have fun as you and your students "master disasters"!

Dinosaurs' Doomsday

Background Information

The extinction of the dinosaurs 65 million years ago is one of science's most intriguing puzzles. For more than 140 million years, these great animals were the dominant life form on earth. Then, practically overnight, the dinosaurs all died.

What killed the dinosaurs? Almost all scientists agree that some change in the earth's environment made the planet uninhabitable for the dinosaurs. Evidence of that change is a layer of iridium, a rare mineral found at the boundary between the Cretaceous and Tertiary geologic periods, coinciding with the death of the dinosaurs.

Scientists fall into two schools of thought on the cause of the environmental change.

Intrinsic gradualists believe that the environmental change was caused by events here on earth, and the change destroyed the dinosaurs over a period of time. The most commonly accepted theory holds that shifts in the earth's tectonic plates caused a series of volcanic eruptions. These eruptions, spewing ash and dust (and iridium) into the atmosphere, might have caused a "greenhouse effect," changing the environment and killing the dinosaurs.

Extrinsic catastrophists believe that some extraterrestrial cause led to the death of the dinosaurs. They point to evidence that a great asteroid more than six miles in diameter struck the earth some 65 million years ago. Such an event, or a series of comets hitting the earth, could have caused a rapid change in the earth's atmosphere and killed the dinosaurs in a short period of time.

The activities in this section will help your students explore the death of the dinosaurs.

What Killed the Dinosaurs?

Science

Introduce the different theories on why dinosaurs became extinct with the comic strip What Killed the Dinosaurs? (pages 9–11). Reproduce and distribute the comic strip to the class, and then have students read the comic aloud. Write words students have trouble with on the chalkboard and review the new vocabulary words with them.

After reading the comic strip, discuss the following questions with the class:

1 What is the boundary between the Cretaceous and the Tertiary layers called? (the K-T Boundary)

2 What is the biggest clue to what killed the dinosaurs? (iridium) What does that clue tell us? (That either an asteroid or comet from outer space collided with Earth, or volcanic eruptions spewed iridium into the atmosphere.)

3 What is the biggest challenge facing scientists who want to learn what killed the dinosaurs? Explain. (Possible answer — the greatest challenge is that all of the clues are found in fossils. This makes it impossible to know with certainty what happened, and there will always be room for different interpretations of what we find in fossils.)

Geologic Time Line

Math, Science

Copy and distribute the Geologic Time Line (page 12), which explains the different periods of the earth's history. To help students comprehend the spans of time shown on the scale, convert one million years to one minute. In that scale...

◈ The earth has been in existence for more than three days.

◈ Dinosaurs arose about four hours ago.

◈ Dinosaurs survived almost three hours— the last one died one hour and five minutes ago.

◈ Human beings have been alive a mere two minutes.

ANSWERS
1. 180 million years
2. 570 million years
3. A.D. 178,000,000

Disaster Lab: Strata Stack

Science

Ask students to suggest ways scientists find dinosaur fossils buried in sedimentary rocks. (By digging; also, fossils are uncovered by erosion or by shifts in the earth's crust caused by earthquakes.) Explain to students that in this activity they will be investigating ways that scientists might count strata of rock to see how old fossils are.

Preparation

Collect old newspapers. You might ask students to bring newspapers from home. Each group of students will need at least two weeks' worth of newspapers, stacked in order from most recent to oldest.

During the Activity

Divide the class into small groups or pairs and distribute copies of Disaster Lab: Strata Stack (page 13) to each group. Have students follow the directions on the reproducible and then observe as they devise ways to find "fossil facts" in the newspapers. As students work, they will discover identifying characteristics on the newspapers, such as thickness, use of color, or easily remembered headlines. Students can also use linear measurements to record how far down in the stack different newspapers are found.

Drawing Conclusions

Have students share their findings with the class. Discuss how the stack of newspapers are like layers of sedimentary rock. (They are stacked according to age, from youngest—near the top—to oldest—near the bottom.) Point out that although rocks do not, of course, have dates printed on them, scientists use scientific methods, such as carbon dating, to determine the age of rocks. This enables them to determine the dates of the different strata of sedimentary rocks.

Find the Craters

(Geography)

This mapping activity challenges students to use lines of longitude and latitude to determine exactly where on earth the doomsday asteroids might have landed, as well as to find well-known dinosaur fossil fields.

Hand out copies of Find the Craters (page 14) and challenge students to locate the craters and dinosaur fossil fields. As students plot the various locations on the map, make sure they recognize that lines of latitude marked *N* are north of the equator and those marked *S* are south of the equator. Longitude lines marked *W* are to the left (west) of the prime meridian, the 0° line of longitude running through England. Longitude marked *E* runs to the right (east) of the prime meridian.

ANSWERS

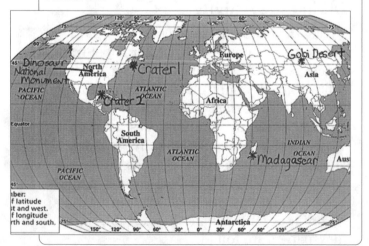

Doomsday Asteroid

(Language Arts)

Reproduce Doomsday Asteroid (page 15) and read the play aloud in class. Discuss the scenario presented in the play and talk about possible solutions. You might ask students if they have seen the movies *Deep Impact* or *Armageddon*, both of which use the doomsday asteroid/comet as their main plot points. Challenge students to come up with different resolutions than the solution used in the movies, in which teams of astronauts managed to divert the "doomsday visitor" with explosives. Point out that scientists have proposed other ways to divert potential doomsday asteroids, such as light-sensitive "sails." When planted on the asteroid, the sails would use the sun's rays to alter the asteroid's course.

Next, invite students to use their imaginations to dream up other ways to divert an asteroid from a collision course with earth, or to imagine the results of such a collision. Then have student use their solutions to complete the play Doomsday Asteroid. Students might work in small groups to complete this project.

For More on Dinosaurs:

DK Pockets: Dinosaurs (DK, 1995). Packed with dinosaur facts and trivia, this minibook is a useful reference to keep on hand during a study of dinosaurs.

Searching for Velociraptor by Lowell Dingus and Mark A Norell (Harpercrest, 1996). This book follows two paleontolgoists on an expedition to find the fossils of the velociraptor dinosaur.

The American Museum of Natural History's Web site (www.amnh.org/science/expeditions/dinosaur/patagonia) features a section with photos and firsthand accounts of a dinosaur fossil hunt in Patagonia.

The National Geographic Web site (www.nationalgeographic.com/dinorama) offers information, as well as multimedia graphics, on dinosaurs.

Dinosaurs' Doomsday, Part 1

For more than 140 million years dinosaurs ruled the earth.
Then, practically overnight...

...the dinosaurs became extinct. The big question: HOW?

Everything we know about dinosaurs, we know from fossils. Fossils, the preserved remains of animals and plants, are usually found buried under the earth's surface. Scientists know the ages of fossils by the layer of rock in which they are found.

"No dinosaurs"

"K-T Boundary"

"Lots and lots of dinosaurs"

The last strata of rock containing dinosaur fossils is called the Cretaceous layer. The next strata is called the Tertiary layer. The break between those layers is called the "K-T Boundary." Something happened at the K-T Boundary to kill half the species alive on earth—including all of the dinosaurs. But what?

Name _____   Date _____

Dinosaurs' Doomsday, Part 2

There have been many theories...

AAAAAA AH-CHOO!!

...Did new types of pollen cause dinosaurs to die of hay fever?

Did mammals steal all of the dinosaur eggs?

...Or did dinosaurs grow so big they couldn't move or feed themselves?

Scientists have rejected all of these theories.
But then....

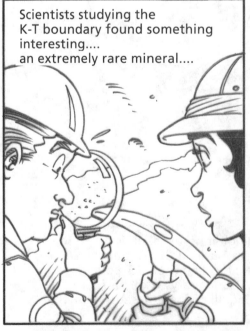

Scientists studying the K-T boundary found something interesting....
an extremely rare mineral....

...IRIDIUM.
The K-T Boundary is lined with it. Iridium, rarely found on the earth's surface, comes from two sources:

Dinosaurs' Doomsday, Part 3

One source is the earth's core. Iridium comes to the surface when volcanoes erupt. The second source is....

Outer space...Iridium comes to Earth on asteroids and meteorites.

Geologists have found two underwater craters. Each crater was made by an asteroid miles wide. They hit the earth 65 million years ago...

Did one or more giant asteroids hit the earth?...

the same time the dinosaurs went extinct!

This caused an environmental disaster... which killed the dinosaurs?

Or is there another possible explanation? What do you think?

Geologic Time Line

The last dinosaur died 65 million years ago. That's a long time...but how long is it compared to the age of the earth? Scientists use a system called the geologic time scale to describe the earth's age.

Cenozoic
65 million years ago to present

◈ Modern mammals

◈ First humans

Paleozoic
570 million to 245 million years ago

◈ Primitive invertebrates and algae

◈ First land plants, fish, and amphibians

◈ First reptiles

◈ Conifers

◈ Insects

Mesozoic
245 million to 65 million years ago

◈ Dinosaurs

◈ Birds

◈ First Mammals

Precambrian
4,568 million to 570 million years ago

◈ Little signs of any life forms

1. How long did dinosaurs live on Earth? _____

2. About how many years ago did the first reptiles appear? _____

3. If humans last as long as dinosaurs, in about what year will humans become extinct? _____

Disasters Scholastic Professional Books

Disaster Lab: Strata Stack

How did the dinosaurs become extinct? The clues are found in fossils. The fossils are found in sedimentary rocks. Sedimentary rocks cover the earth like layers in a cake. Each layer is called a strata. As a rule of thumb, the further down a strata is, the farther back in time it was formed.

What you need:

A stack of old newspapers waiting to be recycled. (Use at least two weeks' worth.)

What you will do:

Design an experiment that shows how scientists count strata of rock to see how old fossils are.

Here's how:

1. Work with a friend. Each of you think of facts you can find in the newspapers. Those facts will be your "fossils." Possible fossils:

   ◈ What was the high temperature last Tuesday?

   ◈ What was the final score of last Wednesday's basketball game?

   ◈ What movies were playing last weekend?

List your "fossils" below.

_____ _____ _____

2. Trade "fossil facts" with your friend. Now, think of ways to find your friend's "fossils" in the stack of newspapers... without looking at the dates of the newspapers.

   ◈ Can you count down from the top of the stack to find the day you are looking for? How about counting up from the bottom?

   ◈ Are there any ways to identify the different layers at a glance? Which day's newspaper is thickest? Which is thinnest? Once you have identified a "landmark" layer, count up or down from it.

3. Find one of your friend's fossil facts in the stack of newspapers. Then put the paper back, making sure the stack is still in order. Let your friend find one of your facts. Take turns finding your "fossils."

   ◈ Does it become easier to find the facts as you go along? Why or why not?

   ◈ Come up with a way to record the "layers" at which you found your "fossil facts." Do not use the dates on the newspapers.

4. Describe your method on the back of this page.

Find the Craters

Geologists have found two huge craters made by giant asteroids that hit the earth about 65 million years ago.

Where are the craters? Use the clues to find and mark them on the map. Then find these famous dinosaur fossil fields.

Crater #1:
The water is warm above this 112-mile-wide crater.

Latitude: 20° N
Longitude: 87° W

Crater #2
This crater, more than 28 miles wide, is in cold seas.

Latitude: 45° N
Longitude: 65° W

Gobi Desert
Latitude: 45° N
Longitude: 110° E

Dinosaur National Monument
Latitude: 41° N
Longitude: 109° W

Madagascar
Latitude: 20° S
Longitude: 47° E

Remember:
Lines of latitude run east and west.
Lines of longitude run north and south.

14

Doomsday Asteroid

CHARACTERS

Jackie
Terry } three friends
Sandy

TV Announcer

Dr. Veronica Jones

First Reporter

Second Reporter

Narrator

Narrator: It's a quiet Saturday afternoon and Jackie, Terry, and Sandy are watching TV at Jackie's house.

Jackie: I'm so bored. Nothing ever happens around here.

Terry: All we ever do is watch TV and play video games.

Sandy: Shhh. Something's happening!

Narrator: Sandy turns up the volume on the TV as an announcer comes on.

TV Announcer: We interrupt our programming for the following special bulletin. We take you now to NASA laboratories in Los Angeles and a press conference with Dr. Veronica Jones, already in progress.

Terry: Hey, Sandy, isn't that Dr. Jones your Aunt Ronnie?

Sandy: Yes. Let's hear what's going on.

Dr. Jones: I repeat, there is no cause for panic. The asteroid will not hit the earth for another six years.

First Reporter: Isn't it true, though, that the asteroid is more than ten miles wide?

Dr. Jones: Yes.

Jackie: Wow! An asteroid that big would....

Narrator: The kids gulp with fear.

Dr. Jones: The impact would be a terrible disaster. It could result in planet-wide fires, earthquakes, volcanic eruptions...we don't know how bad it could be. We are working on plans to stop the asteroid.

First Reporter: How?

Dr. Jones: I can't say. But we are rounding up volunteers to help.

Narrator: At that instant the phone rings. The three friends jump up, startled.

WHAT HAPPENS NEXT?   Finish the story. Write a play describing how the characters face the doomsday asteroid.

The Wrath of Vesuvius

Background Information

When Mount Vesuvius erupted on August 24, A.D. 79, it resulted in one of the greatest disasters in the ancient world. It also proved to be a very significant event for modern scholars.

The ash and pumice spewed from the erupting volcano buried and preserved two Roman towns—Herculaneum and Pompeii—providing historians and archaeologists with perfectly intact examples of daily life in ancient Rome. What's more, the eruption was witnessed by the Roman writer Pliny the Younger, who recorded his observations. Pliny's account includes the story of the death of his heroic uncle, Pliny the Elder, who died attempting to rescue people trapped by the falling ash.

Before you start this unit, ask students what they know about volcanic eruptions. Most will probably have visions of volcanoes spewing red-hot lava. Explain to students that some volcanoes, such as the shield volcanoes in Hawaii, do emit red-hot lava when they erupt. In some volcanic eruptions, however, the magma trapped below the surface is forced out through a narrow vent and turns into ash, pumice, and steam, which is spewed into the air and covers everything in its path.

The following activities will help your students explore the eruption of Mount Vesuvius.

The Wrath of Vesuvius

(Language Arts, Social Studies)

Reproduce and distribute the play The Wrath of Vesuvius (pages 19–24). Tell students that it is based on an eyewitness account of the disaster written by the Roman writer Pliny the Younger, who witnessed the disaster when he was 17 years old. (Since the narrator's role is so large, we suggest that you alternate readers after each scene, giving more than one student the chance to read the narrator's part.)

After reading the play, discuss the following questions with the class.

1 Why does Pliny the Elder at first want to head to Mount Vesuvius? How does his attitude change? What makes him change his attitude? (He is at first curious to see the eruptions, then decides to try to save lives. The letter from his friend, begging for help, changes his attitude.)

2 Would you describe Pliny the Younger as brave or not? Explain. (Possible answer—yes, he is brave, since he refused to leave his mother behind in an attempt to save himself.)

3 Who would you say was braver: Pliny the Elder, who sailed into danger in an attempt to save other people, or his sister, the mother of Pliny the Younger, who offered to give up her life so that her son might escape danger? Explain. (Answers will vary.)

Pliny's Route

(Geography)

This map (page 25) will help students visualize the action of the play. You may wish to reproduce and distribute copies of it before students read the play.

Know Your Volcano

(Science)

Use an apple for a hands-on demonstration of the basic geology of volcanoes. Tell students that if the earth were the size of the apple, the crust would be about the same thickness as the apple's skin. The layer under the earth's crust is called the *mantle*, which is like the white flesh of the apple. The mantle surrounds the earth's core. It is very hot and under intense pressure. The minerals and rocks found there are in liquid (molten) form called *magma*. Volcanoes are formed when magma erupts through the weak or cracked points in the earth's crust.

Next, help students identify the parts of a volcano and the stages of a volcanic eruption by having them complete the Know Your Volcano reproducible (page 26).

ANSWERS

Name _____ Date _____

Know Your Volcano

Read each description. Then draw a line to link each description to the correct part of the diagram.

Cone—the above ground mountain part of a volcano.

Lava—hot molten rock that has flowed to the earth's surface.

Magma—hot molten rock below the earth's surface.

Magma Chamber—the underground pocket where magma gathers beneath the earth's surface.

Vent—the passage from the magma chamber to the surface.

Countdown to Destruction: 4, 2, 5, 1, 3.

Disaster Lab: Model Mount Vesuvius

(Science, Mapping)

In this activity, students use a topologic map to make an accurate three-dimensional model of Mount Vesuvius.

Preparation

Divide the class into small groups. Each group will need sheets of modeling clay, approximately one-quarter- to one-half-inch thick, scissors, butter knives, 2 copies of the Topographical Map (page 28) and the Model Mount Vesuvius reproducible (page 27). Have students cover their desks or work surfaces with newspapers.

During the Activity

Have students follow the directions on Model Mount Vesuvius to create the model pattern using the Topographical Map. Then students can use the pattern to create and assemble the model using the clay. Each student in the group can be responsible for a different task.

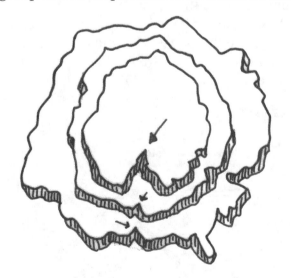

Drawing Conclusions

After students have made their models, challenge them to use their models to make scale drawings of Vesuvius shown from a variety of angles. They can compare their drawings with photos of the volcano.

A Natural Myth

(Language Arts)

Tell students that term volcano comes from Vulcan, a Roman god. According to Roman mythology, Vulcan was the blacksmith for the gods, using a mighty forge to make their weapons and armor. Vulcan was considered hardworking and dull, but given to fits of rage over the antics of his wife, Venus, the goddess of love. Romans believed that Vulcan's forge was beneath the mountain on the island of Vulcano, an active volcano west of Italy.

Challenge students to invent their own god or goddess to explain a natural phenomenon. (Possible choices: tornadoes, solar eclipses, radio/television waves, microwaves.) Have students think of the personal qualities their characters would have. Then let them write an original myth featuring their god or goddess interacting with humans and other gods.

For More on Mount Vesuvius and Volcanoes:

The Buried City of Pompeii by Shelly Tanaka (Disney Press, 1997). A fictional account of the day Mount Vesuvius erupted, plus information about volcanoes and the excavation of Pompeii.

The Day a City Was Buried by Christopher Rice (DK Publishing, 1998). Filled with fascinating facts and information-packed illustrations.

Eyewitness Activity Files: Volcano (DK Publishing, 1999). Includes posters, photos, transcripts, eyewitness accounts, and more.

Volcanoes: Mind-Boggling Experiments You Can Turn Into Science Fair Projects by Janice VanCleave (John Wiley, 1994). Extend your study of volcanoes with the hands-on activities and experiments in this book.

Volcano World Web site's (http://volcano.und.edu/vw.html) features a volcano of the week and fascinating facts about volcanoes.

The Wrath of Vesuvius

This play is based on an eyewitness report of the eruption of Vesuvius. The great volcano erupted on August 24, 79 A.D.. The eruption of Vesuvius was one of the greatest disasters of the ancient world. It was also the first major eruption to be described in detail by an eyewitness.

The famous Roman writer Pliny the Younger lived near Mount Vesuvius at the time of the eruption. He was 17 years old when the disaster occurred. His uncle, Pliny the Elder, was a well-known writer and soldier. Pliny the Younger described the eruption of Vesuvius in a letter to the historian Tacitus.

CHARACTERS

Pliny the Younger

Pliny the Elder, his uncle

Mother

Helmsman

Pomponianus

Sailor #1

Sailor #2

Lucius

Man #1

Man #2

Man #3

Man #4

Narrator (Pliny the Younger, looking back at what happened during the eruption of Vesuvius.)

SCENE ONE

Narrator: My dear Tacitus. You ask me to write you something about the recent disaster, so that the account you write is as reliable as possible. It was on the twenty-fourth of August. I was with my uncle and mother at his villa in Misenum, a port town to the north of Mount Vesuvius. At about two o'clock in the afternoon on that fateful day, my uncle was relaxing with his books after he had his bath. My mother came into his study....

Mother: Brother, come quickly. There's a strange cloud rising in the sky.

Pliny the Elder: Yes?

Narrator: My mother and uncle went to the patio overlooking the harbor. Behind them, rising above Mount Vesuvius, was a huge gray cloud.

Pliny the Elder: It looks like a giant gray tree trunk, with branches spreading out from the top.

Mother: What do you think has caused it?

Pliny the Elder: I don't know. But it might have something to do with the earth tremors we have felt these past few mornings. I'll go and explore. Ask the servants to prepare a boat. We will sail to the base of Vesuvius.

Narrator: My uncle came into my room, where I was working at my studies.

Pliny the Elder: Nephew, something is happening on Mount Vesuvius. Do you want to come see it with me?

Pliny the Younger: I'm sorry, Uncle. The writing exercise you gave me is more interesting than anything I would see on the mountain.

Pliny the Elder (*laughing*): You are a true scholar!

Narrator: My uncle agreed to let me stay behind. As he was preparing to leave, a messenger arrived with a letter.

Pliny the Elder: What message is this?

Mother: It's from our friend, Rectina.

Pliny the Elder: She lives in the shadows of Vesuvius. What does she write?

Mother (*reading*): "My friends, help us! Everything here is in turmoil. All roads are blocked by falling ashes. Our only hope is to escape by boat. If my servant gets through to you with this letter, I beg you to come and save us."

Pliny the Elder (*grimly*): Is my boat ready?

Servant: It is, sir.

Pliny the Elder: Good. I thought this would be an educational trip. Now I see that much more is at stake.

SCENE TWO

Narrator: My uncle took command of his boat.

Pliny the Elder: Head toward the bay at the foot of Mount Vesuvius.

Helmsman: But all of the other boats there are leaving the bay. Why should we go where others are fleeing?

Pliny the Elder: To help others, and to learn.

Narrator: The boat made its way toward Mount Vesuvius. My uncle called a scribe to his side. He described what he saw. The scribe wrote it all down.

Pliny the Elder: The evil cloud above Mount Vesuvius is growing larger and larger. The entire sky is blackened by it. The cloud seems to be made of ash, which is falling from the sky like heavy snow. Rocks, blackened by fire, drop like meteors from the sky into the water.

Helmsman: Sir! We cannot get to the shore on this side of the bay. The ash and rocks are filling the ocean—the water near the shore is too shallow for our boat. I beg you—let's turn back while we have the chance!

Narrator: My uncle watched the cloud of falling ash. He heard the faint cries of people on the far shore.

Pliny the Elder: Fortune favors the brave.

Head for the far shore!

Narrator: The boat made its way across the bay to the other shore.

SCENE THREE

Narrator: My uncle's boat headed for the docks at the town of Stabiae. His friend, Pomponianus, had his boats loaded at the docks there. He paced, nervous, as the ash fell from the sky.

Pomponianus: We must get away as soon as possible.

Sailor #1: We will, sir, as soon as the wind stops blowing in from the sea.

Sailor #2: Look, sir. The wind is blowing another ship to our docks.

Sailor #1: Who would defy death by sailing into this awful place?

Pomponianus: It's Pliny.

Narrator: My uncle's boat docked, and he embraced his terrified friend.

Pomponianus: Pliny, why have you come? You could have used your ship to escape.

Pliny the Elder: And leave my friends behind?

Pomponianus: I'm afraid it's too late for any of us to escape now.

Pliny the Elder: My friend, every person alive must die sooner or later.

Narrator: My uncle stared at the falling cloud of ash. It was lit by great flashes of lightning.

Pliny the Elder: Everyone must die...but very few of us get to see such an amazing sight as this. Come on, we'll be safe in your house.

Pomponianus: Yes...but for how long?

SCENE FOUR

Narrator: While my Uncle traveled to the very foot of Vesuvius, my mother and I tried to carry on our normal lives. I finished up my studies. I had a bath, then dinner. Then I went to bed—but of course, I could not sleep. In the middle of the night, the ground began to shake violently. My mother rushed into my room.

Mother: Son! Wake up!

Pliny the Younger: I haven't been sleeping. Who can sleep while the world is ending?

Mother: Do you think that's what's happening?

Pliny the Younger (*laughing*): Of course not. I'm only joking. Let's go out on the terrace. From there I'll be able to keep an eye on what's happening while you get some sleep. I'll wake you if need be.

Narrator: We went to the terrace. My mother rested as I watched the great column of ash grow over Vesuvius. Since there was nothing to do but wait, I got my book and resumed studying. And that's how we were when Lucius, a friend of my uncle's arrived.

Lucius: What's this? One of you sleeping, the other one reading, even as the heavens rain fire?

Narrator: By this time, the sun had come up to reveal an eerie, gray morning. The gray cloud above Vesuvius was flashing with lightning and sheets of flame.

Mother: What should we do?

Lucius: Come with me...now!

Pliny the Younger: But we're miles from Vesuvius. What could happen to us here?

Narrator: The ground shook violently. It was the worst tremor we had ever felt. It seemed as if the house would collapse on our heads. Then, as suddenly as it began, the tremor stopped.

Mother: I agree with Lucius. Let's go!

Narrator: We hastily packed some things and made our way out of Misenum. We joined a crowd of others streaming for the city gates.

SCENE FIVE

Narrator: We headed along the shore, where we saw a bizarre sight. The sea seemed to be sucked away from the shore. Many sea creatures were left flopping on the sand. And behind us, the column of flame and ash grew higher and higher.

Mother: I can't go on much longer. Son, save yourself. You're young. You can make it. Leave me behind. I will die happy if I know that I wasn't the cause of your death.

Lucius (*to Pliny the Younger*): She's right. We should save ourselves.

Narrator: I looked behind my mother. The cloud was lower now, and was rolling across the land and sea. Towns along the coast seemed to vanish in the cloud. Our own hometown, Misenum, was lost in the gray cloud.

Pliny the Younger: Give me your hand, Mother. We can both move a little faster.

Lucius: Fool!

Narrator: Lucius ran off into the darkness. We never saw him again.

22

SCENE SIX

Narrator: I helped my mother pick up her pace. As we struggled along, a thin dust began to fall from above like a gentle flurry of snow. I turned again—a dense cloud of ash was rolling across the land, like a flood surging after us. Other people on the road saw the cloud, too.

Man #1: Here it comes!

Man #2: The end is here! Run for your lives!

Narrator: The crowd of people leaving Misenum began to panic.

Pliny the Younger: Mother, come on!

Narrator: We turned off the road before the rushing crowd crushed us. As we waited for the fleeing mob to pass, a darkness came. It was not like a moonless or cloudy night, but more like the black of closed and unlit rooms. I clutched my mother's hand as the thick ash fell.

SCENE SEVEN

Narrator: Meanwhile, my uncle had spent the night at his friend's villa. By morning, the house was being rocked on its foundations by violent tremors.

Pomponianus: Should we leave? The building will surely collapse!

Narrator: From the roof came a constant knocking sound.

Pliny the Elder: Do you hear that?

Pomponianus: What could it be?

Pliny the Elder: Rocks. The sky is raining stones and ashes. If we go out, we could be buried alive or crushed.

Pomponianus: What should we do?

Narrator: My uncle thought about the options.

Pliny the Elder: Let's head for the shore. Maybe our boats are still afloat. We have a chance to escape there—here we face certain death.

Narrator: My uncle and the others tied pillows to their heads as protection against the shower of rock. Using torches, they made their way to the shore.

Pomponianus: It's darker than midnight. The sun should have come up hours ago.

Pliny the Elder: I'm afraid it did come up...and is shining on the rest of the world, but not on us.

Narrator: At last, they made it to the shore.

Pliny the Elder (*gasping for breath*): The sea...is too rough. We...cannot...escape.

Narrator: The smell of sulfur filled the air. Walls of flame rolled from the darkness toward the sea.

Man #3: Run for it!

Narrator: The younger, stronger men ran with all of their might along the shore away from the disaster. My uncle, his nose and mouth filled with ash and dust, collapsed to the ground. His body remains there to this day.

SCENE EIGHT

Narrator: My mother and I sat silently in pitch darkness as, all around us, ash continued to fall. We could hear the voices of frightened, lost souls.

Man #4: Help me! I...can't...breath!

Mother: Son? Son! Look! There's a light in the distance! Is it the sun?

Narrator: My mother was filled with hope at the approaching light. But I knew better.

Pliny the Younger: Mother, that's not the sun. It's fire. We must get out of here!

Narrator: Somehow we plowed our way through the ash. The slowly creeping fire at our backs lit the way. An even heavier cloud of ashes fell on our heads. My mother collapsed, exhausted.

Mother: Save yourself.

Narrator: Without a word, I lifted my mother to her feet. Had she remained on the ground, she would have certainly been buried alive.

SCENE NINE

Narrator: At last, the falling ash began to thin out. A pale gray light glowed all around us.

Pliny the Younger: It's the sun. The sun! Mother, we did it. We survived!

Narrator: The light grew stronger, but with a lurid glow, as after an eclipse. It showed us a changed world — a world buried in ash like snow. The earth was still quaking. In the distance, Vesuvius loomed, the gray cloud above it lit with a terrifying orange glow.

Pliny the Younger: We should head back to town. Perhaps our house is saved. Maybe my uncle made it back. Maybe everything will be the same as it was before....

Narrator: My mother put a hand to my lips. A sorry smile crossed her face.

Mother: No, son. No. Nothing will ever be the same.

EPILOGUE

The eruption of Vesuvius in A.D. 79 buried two towns, Herculaneum and Pompeii, in ash and cinders, which later turned to solid rock. Thousands of people were buried alive in the disaster.

Vesuvius is still an active volcano. It has had dozens of eruptions in the years since 79. The most recent eruption was in 1944.

To this day, people live in the shadows of Vesuvius.

Pliny's Route

This map shows the route Pliny the Elder took during the eruption of Mount Vesuvius.

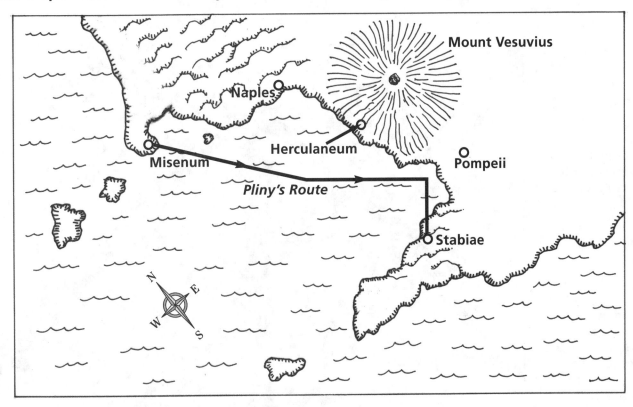

1. What basic direction did Pliny take? _____

2. Where did Pliny end up? _____

3. Name at least two towns Pliny passed on his journey.

   _____

4. Name the town just about due south of Mount Vesuvius.

   _____

   Herculaneum was buried under almost 300 meters of volcanic ash.
   Pompeii was buried in 50 meters of ash. Most of the city of Naples
   escaped destruction.

5. Based on this information, in which direction would you say was the path of
   greatest destruction? Explain.

   _____

   _____

   _____

Know Your Volcano

Read each description. Then draw a line to link each description to the correct part of the diagram.

Cone—the above ground mountain part of a volcano.

Lava—hot molten rock that has flowed to the earth's surface.

Magma—hot molten rock below the earth's surface.

Magma Chamber—the underground pocket where magma gathers beneath the earth's surface.

Vent—the passage from the magma chamber to the surface.

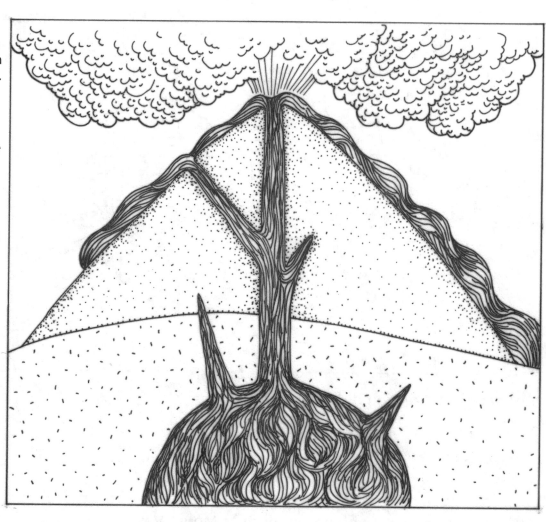

COUNTDOWN TO DESTRUCTION

Use the numbers 1 to 5 to put the following stages of an eruption in correct order.

____ Ash, cinders, and lava are spewed from the vent.

____ Boiling hot gases build up and increase the pressure inside the magma chamber. The pressure builds...and builds...and builds....

____ Layers of ash and lava give the volcano a different shape.

____ The volcano is dormant, or inactive. Its vent is blocked by rocks.

____ The building pressure unblocks the vent. Often, this happens with a tremendous explosion.

Disasters Scholastic Professional Books

Model Mount Vesuvius

You can make a three-dimensional model of Mount Vesuvius. Here's how.

You'll Need:
- sheets of modeling clay
- topographic map of Mount Vesuvius
- scissors
- butter knife

STEP 1

Use the topographic map of Mount Vesuvius to create the six layers of your model. The lines show intervals of 200 meters as you go up Mount Vesuvius. Everything along a line is at the same altitude. It's like layers on a cake, with the layers getting smaller as you go up. CAREFULLY cut out the map.

STEP 2

Place the map on a piece of modeling clay. CAREFULLY cut the clay in the shape of the map. Make a notch in the clay below the horizontal line marked on the pattern. You'll use these notches to stack up the layers.

STEP 3

Carefully cut off the first ring on the map. Place the map on the piece of modeling clay. Carefully cut the clay in the shape of the map. Continue until you have created all six layers of the model.

STEP 4

Make your mountain!
When you have cut out all six layers, stack them up. Refer to an original, uncut copy of the map to make sure you get each layer in the correct position. Press them together as you stack up your layers.

How does your model "stack up"? Compare it with photos of the real Mount Vesuvius.

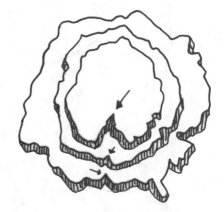

Topographical Map

Use this topographical map to create a model of Mount Vesuvius.

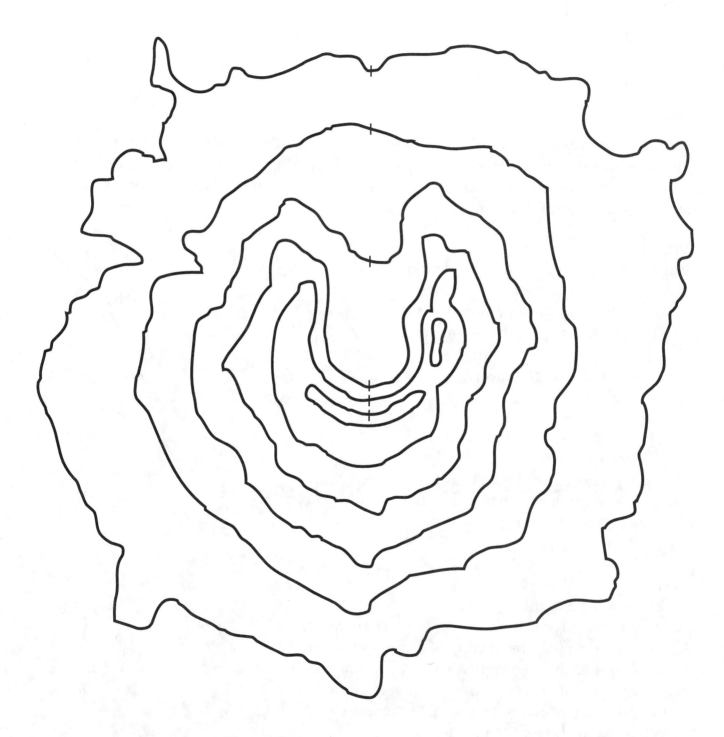

Disasters Scholastic Professional Books

The Johnstown Flood

Background Information

On May 31, 1889, a storm brought heavy rain to Johnstown, Pennsylvania. Because of the rain, the water in nearby Lake Conemaugh rose, breaking the South Fork Dam and releasing a wall of water that destroyed the town of Johnstown.

The Johnstown Flood was one of the most devastating disasters in American history and it was an important historical event on many levels. First and foremost, it was one of the greatest single disasters in American history, resulting in terrible loss of life. The fact that the tragedy was caused by a poorly maintained dam owned by a group of arrogant millionaires helped to spur social reform throughout the 1890s and beyond. Finally, the Johnstown Flood was one of the first major events covered by the growing news media.

Use the six reproducible student pages to tell the tragic story of the Johnstown Flood to your students. Following are suggested projects and activities linked to the pages.

The Great Debate

(Social Studies)

After students have read The Situation (page 33), divide the class into two teams and have them debate the following proposition:

"Resolved: The South Fork Fishing and Hunting Club should be forced to drain its lake."

One group of students should take the position in favor of this statement, and the other group should oppose it. Suggest the following arguments for each side to consider:

In favor of draining the lake

◆ Johnstown is in danger, given the size of the lake and the steepness of the mountains surrounding the area.

◆ It is unfair to allow only 66 people to use the lake.

◆ The lake has no useful purpose.

In favor of keeping the lake

◆ It is good for the valley to have rich people visit there.

◆ The dam was built by the state and is very large, so it must be safe.

◆ The *Johnstown Tribune* does not think that the dam is dangerous.

Make a Scale Drawing

(Math)

Have students make a scale drawing of the lake and the dam holding it back using the information on the reproducible The Situation. Students will need graph paper and pencils for this activity.

First, have students convert the size of the lake from miles to feet. Compare the size of the lake with the length of the dam. (One mile equals 5,280 feet. The lake is 5,280 feet wide and about 10,560 feet long. The dam is 900 feet wide.)

Next, ask students to round the distances to easy-to-use numbers. (For instance, 900 feet rounds up to 1,000 feet; 5,280 rounds down to 5,250 feet; and 10,560 rounds down to 10,500.)

Now have students create a scale for their drawings. For instance, they could use a scale of 1,000 feet to 1 square. In that case, the dam would be 1 square long. How wide would the lake be? (5 and 1/4 squares) How long would it be? (10 and 1/2 squares) Allow students to use more accurate scales if they wish.

What's the Rate?

(Math)

Have students use their math skills and information found on the reproducibles The Situation and Memorial Day, 1889, to answer this question:

At the rate the rain fell on May 31, 1889, how long did it take for the water level in Lake Conemaugh to rise over the top of the dam?

To answer this question, students should break it down into a series of steps.

Step One: Find the Necessary Facts

First Fact—How far did the water have to rise before it went over the dam? To find this, subtract the height of the dam from the depth of the lake. The dam was 72 feet high, and the lake was 60 feet deep. 72 − 60 = 12. The water would have to rise 12 feet.

Second Fact—How fast did the rain fall? It fell at a rate that raised the water level in the lake one inch every ten minutes.

Step Two: Use the Numbers to Write A Problem

Suggest that students work backward from what they know to what they want to find out.

For example: "The distance from the surface to the top of the dam is 12 feet. The level rises 1 inch every 10 minutes. In how many minutes will the level reach the top?"

Step Three: Solve the Problem

One strategy to suggest is to convert the number to common units. In this case, convert the rate at which the water rises from inches to feet. The water rises 1 inch in 10 minutes. There are 12 inches in 1 foot. Therefore, it would take 120 minutes, or 2 hours, for the water to rise 1 foot. At the rate of 1 inch every 10 minutes, it would take 24 hours for the water level to rise 12 feet.

The Breaking Story

(Language Arts)

Ask students to imagine that modern media, such as television and radio, existed back in 1889. Then have students work in small groups to write and deliver on-the-spot news reports of the Johnstown Flood, using the information on the student pages. Have them consider incorporating the following news practices in their stories:

- ◇ Interviews with eyewitnesses
- ◇ "Expert" commentary
- ◇ Charts, diagrams, and other graphics
- ◇ Reenactments

On Trial!

(Social Studies)

After students are familiar with the story of the Johnstown Flood, stage a mock trial of the South Fork Fishing and Hunting Club. Assign students to act as two teams of lawyers. One team of lawyers is suing the South Fork Hunting and Fishing Club on behalf of a group of the flood's victims. (They are the *plaintiffs*.) The other lawyers defend the club. (They are the *defendants*.) Assign a student to be the judge, and select 12 others

to be the jury. Assign other students roles as witnesses, including:

- ◇ Editor of the *Johnstown Tribune*
- ◇ Eyewitnesses to the dam break
- ◇ Eyewitnesses to the destruction of the flood
- ◇ Medical experts to report on the destruction of the flood

To prepare for the trial, students should conduct research into the Johnston Flood, uncovering additional facts and information to support their cases. (See Resources on page 32 for book and Web site suggestions.) Stage the trial in the following sequence:

Opening arguments: Each team of lawyers tells the jury what to expect in the trial.

Plaintiff's case: The team of lawyers suing the club call their witnesses and ask each witness questions about the flood and the club's role in its cause. In each case, the defendant's lawyers get to cross-examine the witnesses.

Defendant's case: The defendant's lawyers get to call witnesses, if they chose. As before, the other team of lawyers gets to cross-examine each witness.

Summations: Each team of lawyers sum up their cases for the jury.

Deliberation: The jury, alone, weighs the evidence and comes to a decision as to whether or not the club is responsible for the flood. In a civil lawsuit, only a majority of the jurors must vote in the plaintiff's favor in order for the defendant to be liable.

Damages: If the jury decides to support the plaintiff, the jury then decides "damages." It comes up with a dollar amount that the defendants must pay the plaintiffs, taking into account how serious the injury was and the amount that the plaintiff is able to pay.

A Memorial Poem

(Language Arts)

The great American poet Walt Whitman wrote the following verse in memory of the Johnstown Flood. Share it with your students after they have read The Aftermath (page 38).

A voice from Death, solemn and strange, in all his sweep and power,

With sudden, indescribable blow—towns drown'd—humanity by thousands slain,

The vaunted work of thrift, goods, dwellings, forge, street, iron bridge,

Dash'd pell-mell by the blow—yet usher'd life continuing on,...

Discuss the following questions with students after reading:

1 What "indescribable blow" is Whitman talking about? (the Johnstown Flood)

2 Does "the vaunted work of thrift" refer to the people who died or the things destroyed by the flood? (the things destroyed)

3 Would you call this a sad or a hopeful poem? (Possible answer: hopeful, since it ends by saying that despite everything, life goes on.)

Challenge students to write a poem in memory of the Johnstown Flood.

For More on the Johnstown Flood:

The Day it Rained Forever: A Story of the Johnstown Flood by Virginia T. Gross (Puffin, 1993). Part of the "Once Upon America" series, a fictionalized account of the flood told from the perspective of a young narrator.

The Flood Disaster by Peg Kehret (Minstrel Books, 1999). Two friends travel back in time to Johnstown, Pennsylvania just before the flood.

The Johnstown Flood by David McCullough (Touchstone Books, 1987). A noteworthy and comprehensive account of the flood. An excellent resource for teachers.

The Johnstown Flood National Memorial's Web site (http://www.nps.gov/jofl/home.htm) provides a wealth of information on the flood, including the transcripts of interviews with eyewitnesses to the disaster.

The Situation

May, 1889

JOHNSTOWN

Founded: 1804

Population: 30,000 people

Location: The Allegheny Mountains in western Pennsylvania.

Facts: Johnstown is nestled in a valley among mountains. The surrounding mountains are so high that a visitor once said, "In Johnstown, the sun rises at ten and sets at two." In 1889, Johnstown is a booming town. The town has tripled in size in less than 20 years.

SOUTH FORK FISHING AND HUNTING CLUB

Founded: 1879

Members: 66 of the richest men in America

Location: Lake Conemaugh, in the mountains above Johnstown

Facts: Lake Conemaugh is a man-made lake 14 miles from Johnstown. It was formed by a dam built on the Little Conemaugh River. The dam was originally built by the state of Pennsylvania. The club repaired the dam when they bought the lake and the land surrounding it in 1879. The dam is 72 feet high and 900 feet wide. The lake behind it is two miles long, a mile wide, and 60 feet deep. The lake is used by the 66 club members as a private place to fish.

PENNSYLVANIA

Pittsburgh
•

• Johnstown

IS THE DAM SAFE?

From the *Johnstown Tribune*:

"We do not consider there is much cause for alarm, as even in the event of the [dam] breaking there is plenty of room for the water to spread out before reaching here, and no damage...would result."

From a report by structural engineers, commissioned by Dan Morrell, the head of the Cambira Iron Company:

"There appear to me two serious elements of danger in the dam: First the want of a discharge pipe to reduce or take the water out of the dam for needed repairs. Second, the unsubstantial method of repair, leaving a large leak, which appears to be cutting the new embankment. ... Should this break [in the dam] be made during a season of flood, it is evident that considerable damage would ensue along the line of the Conemaugh. "

Memorial Day, 1889

WEATHER REPORT

On Tuesday, May 28, a huge storm forms over Kansas and Nebraska. Hard rain falls from Michigan to Tennessee. Tornado-like winds kill several people in Kansas. The storm moves into Pennsylvania.

IN JOHNSTOWN....

Up to six inches of rain fall by noon on May 31. The town is flooded, as nearby rivers overflow their banks. The water in town ranges from two feet to ten feet deep.

From the *Johnstown Tribune*, May 31, 1889

"As we write at noon, Johnstown is again under water, and all about us the tide is rising. Wagons for hours have been passing along the streets carrying people from submerged points to places of safety....At three o'clock, the town sat down with its hands in its pockets to make the best of a dreary situation."

ON LAKE CONEMAUGH:

The rain falls even harder on Lake Conemaugh. The level of the lake rises at the rate of one inch every ten minutes. Soon the surface of the water is near the top of the dam.

At 2:30 p.m., the engineer at the dam sends a telegraph to Johnstown, located 14 miles down the winding valley:

"THE DAM IS BECOMING DANGEROUS AND MAY POSSIBLY GO."

3:10 p.m., Friday, May 31, 1889

A group of men watch nervously as water begins to pour over the top of the dam holding back Lake Conemaugh. Their eyewitness reports:

"It ran over a short spell...and then it just cut through like a knife."

"It ran over the top until it cut a channel, and then it ran out as fast as it could get out. It went out very fast, but it didn't burst out...."

"Water worked its way down little by little, until it got a little headway, and when it got cut through it just went like a flash."

"The whole dam seemed to push out all at once. No, not a break, just one big push."

In a split second, the dam melts away. Twenty million tons of water surge down the valley. It is as if Niagara Falls has been suddenly unleashed on the valley. **The wall of water, 40 feet high, heads straight for Johnstown.**

The Johnstown Flood, Part 1

Use the map below and the descriptions on The Johnstown Flood, Part 2 to follow the path of the flood.

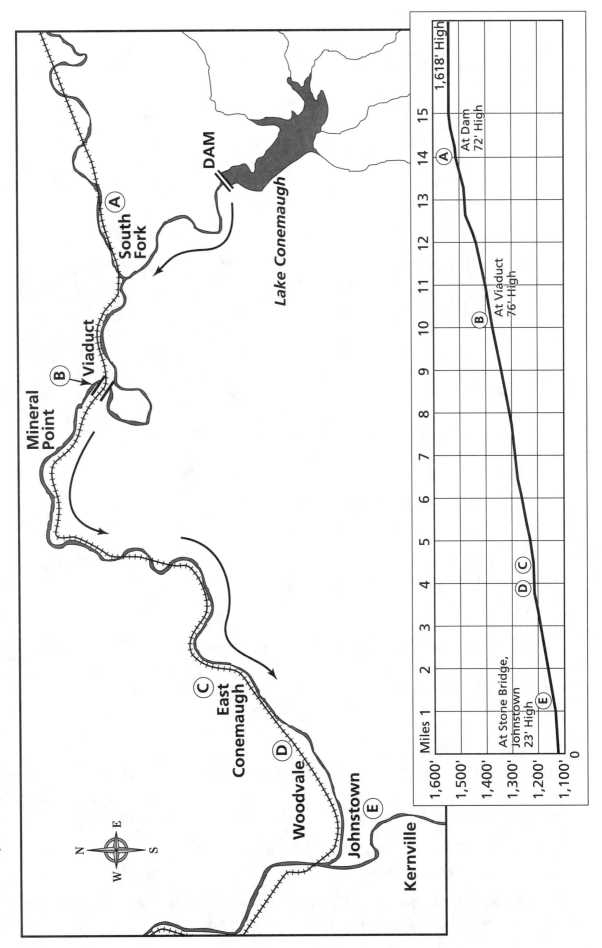

The Johnstown Flood, Part 2

A. SOUTH FORK

"It looked like a mountain coming."
— Emma Ehrenfeld

First flood fatality: Michael Mann. His body is found ten days later, buried in mud a mile and a half downstream.

B. VIADUCT

The valley narrows here. The wall of water grows to 75 feet in height. It runs into a strong stone bridge, called a viaduct. For a few minutes, the water stops here. Pressure behind it grows and grows. Then, in a flash, the bridge collapses. The water surges down the valley with more force than ever.

C. EAST CONEMAUGH

Dozens of train cars wait out the storm in a train station. Then, at about quarter to four, people at the station see the thirty-foot tall wall of water. It washes through the town and station. Entire train cars were swept from their tracks.

"The trains looked like toys in the hands of a giant."
— Eyewitness

Forty houses are swept away. Thirty locomotives, each weighing as much as 80 tons, are also carried off. At least 50 people are killed.

D. WOODVALE

The entire town is wiped off the map. Not a house, not a store, not a tree is left standing.

A wire factory is destroyed. Miles of razor-sharp barbed wire is carried along with the other debris on the wall of water.

Three hundred and fourteen people die in Woodvale— one-third of its entire population.

E. JOHNSTOWN

At 4 p.m., the rain is slowing in Johnstown. The sky brightens. Most people think the worst is over.

Then, the wall of water hits the town. According to eyewitnesses:

"First, there was a roar like thunder."
"It was like a great fire, the dust it raised."
"It crushed houses like eggshells."

The wave sweeps through Johnstown, destroying everything in its path.

At the western end of town, the water slams into a stone bridge. The water, clogged with trees, houses, and bodies, stops there. Upstream, Johnstown is buried under 23 feet of water. More than 1,000 people drown or are crushed.

At the stone bridge, the pile of debris is soaked in train diesel fuel. Sparks from charcoal stoves start a fire. Soon, the debris burns out of control. Flames trap more than 80 people, who burn to death in the midst of a flood.

The Aftermath

NUMBER OF DEATHS IN THE JOHNSTOWN FLOOD

2,209 people killed

99 entire families dead

396 children under the age of ten die

98 children lost both parents

777 unidentified victims

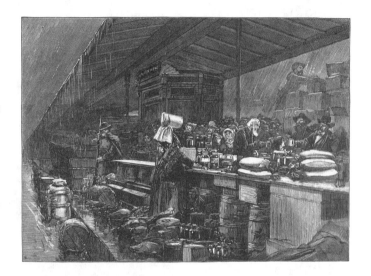

PROPERTY DAMAGE

$17 million in property destroyed

1,600 homes destroyed

280 businesses ruined

Quote:

"A rat caught in a trap and placed in a bucket would not be more helpless than we were."

—Johnstown Tribune

RELIEF EFFORTS

The world was shocked by the Johnstown Flood. People from all over sent money and goods to help the victims. Some sample contributions:

Money

$1,136.93	*Nantucket, Massachusetts*
$101	*Tombstone, Arizona*
$20,000	*New York Stock Exchange*
$300	*President William Henry Harrison*

Supplies

20,000 pounds of ham	*City of Cincinnati*
1,000 loaves of bread	*Prisoners of Western Penitentiary*
Train car full of nails	*Wheeling, West Virginia*
16 train cars of flour	*Minneapolis, Minnesota*
1,000 blankets	*South Fork Fishing and Hunting Club*

Total Donations: $3,742,818.78

WHO WAS TO BLAME?

Many victims sued the South Fork Fishing and Hunting Club, claiming it was to blame for the disaster. In every case, juries found the Club not guilty. The verdict?

The Johnstown Flood was "an act of God."

What do you think?

The Death of the *Titanic*

Background Information

The sinking of the *Titanic* on April 15, 1912, is perhaps the most famous disaster in history. The following student play takes a unique approach to the well-known disaster.

The play is based on the U.S. Senate investigation into the disaster, which began within days of the survivors' arrival in the United States. The thorough investigation, led by Senator William Alden Smith, established the facts of the *Titanic*'s demise, providing us with a solid historical record of the event. It also resulted in many new laws and regulations that made ship travel far safer than before.

The Death of the Titanic is followed by a fact sheet which provides more information on the ship and the disaster, plus additional student reproducibles.

The Death of the *Titanic*

(Language Arts, Social Studies)

Copy and distribute the play and the *Titanic* Facts. After reading the play aloud in class, use the following questions to spur discussion.

1 **Scene One:** Maggie and the Senator Page discuss rumors of the *Titanic* days after the ship sank. They are not yet sure of exactly what happened on the ship. How would the scene be different if an accident like the *Titanic* happened today?

2 **Scene Three:** Why do you think Ismay turned his back on the sinking *Titanic*? If it were up to him, do you think the disaster would have been investigated? Why or why not?

3 **Scene Four:** Why does Captain Smith think the *Titanic* does not need to slow down, despite the warnings of ice ahead?

4 **Scene Five:** Do you agree with Fleet's excuse for the lack of binoculars for the lookouts? Explain. What is Fleet's initial reaction when the *Titanic* scrapes the iceberg? According to Fleet's testimony, how could the *Titanic* have avoided the iceberg?

5 **Scene Eight:** Why do you think the *Titanic*'s designers did not seal off the top of the watertight compartments? What does that tell you about their opinion of the ship's safety?

6 **Scene Nine:** What is the reaction of the passengers when the crew tells them to get into the lifeboats? How do you think that affected the number of people who ended up dying in the disaster?

7 **Scene Ten:** Why did so many third-class passengers miss the chance to get off the ship in lifeboats?

8 **Scene Eleven:** Why did the people in the half-empty lifeboats choose not to go back to help the people freezing to death in the water? Do you think they were justified? Explain.

9 **Scene Twelve:** What was Captain Lord's excuse for not helping the *Titanic*? Do you think it is valid? Explain.

10 **Scene Fourteen:** What does Senator Smith learn when he visits the *Olympic*? Of all the things that led to the *Titanic*'s sinking, which cause do you think would have been the easiest one to avoid? Explain.

The Deadly Toll

(Math)

To help students visual the survival rate among the *Titanic*'s passengers in First Class, Second Class, Third Class, and crew, have them complete the graphing activity on The Deadly Toll reproducible (page 58).

ANSWERS
1. Second Class   3. Third Class
2. First Class   4. Three

Send an SOS

(Science)

Before students complete the Send an SOS reproducible (page 59), explain that the first "wireless sets," such as the one used on the *Titanic*, sent electric signals over radio waves. It was up to the wireless operators to translate those signals into messages.

Have students write their messages in the classroom, then allow them to send their messages in the school yard or playground. Students can experiment with different media for their Morse code messages. An obvious way to send the messages is by flashing them with flashlights. Students can also convey their messages aurally by using whistles or horns.

Disaster Lab: Sink the Ship

(Science)

This activity demonstrates how the *Titanic*'s watertight compartments filled with water in sequence, dragging the ship down.

Preparation

Have students work in teams. Each team will need a copy of Disaster Lab: Sink the Ship (page 60), two aluminum-foil muffin pans, paper fasteners, coins or other small weights, a pen, and a sink or basin of water.

During the Activity

Have students construct the model following the directions on the reproducible. Make sure students poke holes in their models large enough to admit water (there will not be enough pressure to break the surface tension and force water through smaller holes). Ask students what causes the compartments not damaged to eventually fill with water. (The weight of the water in the damaged compartments drags the model down lower in the water, allowing water to spill into the intact compartments.) How does the "cargo" affect the model? (As the model sinks lower in the water, the cargo shifts forward. This adds to the weight in the front of the model, causing it to sink even faster.)

Drawing Conclusions

Have students draw up a list of design changes that could have prevented the *Titanic* from sinking. (Sealing off the tops of the watertight compartments; having a double hull; increasing the number of watertight compartments; etc.) Students might create a new model to test their design ideas.

For More on the *Titanic*:

Exploring the Titanic by Robert Ballard (Scholastic, 1993). Tells the complete story of the sinking of the *Titanic* and Robert Ballard's journey to the bottom of the sea to explore the wreckage of this great ship.

On Board the Titanic by Shelley Tanaka, illustrated by Ken Marschall (Hyperion/Madision Press, 1996). Told through the eyes of two survivors, a riveting account of the last hours of the *Titanic*.

Titanic: An Illustrated History by Donald Lynch (Hyperion, 1998). An in-depth account of the *Titanic*, with illustrations by Ken Marschall

The Titanic Sinks by Thomas Conklin (Random House, 1997). A nonfiction account of the disaster based on eyewitness reports.

Voyage on the Great Titanic: The Diary of Margaret Ann Brady (Scholastic, 1998). Part of the "Dear America" series, a fictionalized account of the tragedy.

The Death of the *Titanic*

When the *Titanic* set sail on its first voyage from Europe to the United States, it was the greatest ship in history. It stood 11 stories tall and stretched longer than 3 football fields. Built of iron and powered by huge steam engines, the ship was the last word in comfort and safety.

There were 899 crew members and officers to run the ship. In first class, 329 passengers settled into cabins as fine as rooms in an elegant hotel. In second class, 285 passengers bought tickets for a comfortable journey across the ocean. And 710 passengers—many of them entire families—traveled in third class. Most of the passengers in third class were emigrants leaving Europe to start a new life in America.

Most of the passengers and crew of the *Titanic* never made it to America. When the ship struck an iceberg and sank early in the morning on April 15, 1912, the entire world was shocked by the news. There were wild rumors about what really happened on the ship.

Today we know most of the details of that fateful night. Much of what we know about the sinking of the *Titanic* is due to the efforts of one man: U.S. Senator William Alden Smith.

Soon after the great ship sank, Smith organized an investigation into the tragedy. He and a team of other senators interviewed survivors within days of the disaster, while their memories were still fresh. All along, Smith wanted to find the answers to two questions:

Why did the Titanic sink? And how could the disaster have been prevented?

CAST OF CHARACTERS

Senator William Alden Smith
Maggie Molloy (his aide)
Senate Page
J. Bruce Ismay, owner of the *Titanic*
Thomas Andrews, designer of
   the *Titanic*

OFFICERS AND CREW OF THE *TITANIC*
Captain E.J. Smith
Charles Lightoller
William Murdoch
Frederick Fleet
Reginald Lee
James Moody
Joseph Boxhall
Harold Lowe
Herbert Pitman
Helmsman
Seaman # 1
Seaman # 2
Seaman # 3
Seaman # 4
Seaman # 5

THE TITANIC'S TELEGRAPH OPERATORS
Harold Bride
Jack Phillips

PASSENGERS ON THE *TITANIC*
Benjamin Hart
Esther Hart
Eva Hart
Archibald Gracie
Female Passenger
Woman
First Man
Second Man
Man in Tuxedo

OFFICERS OF THE *CALIFORNIAN*
Captain Stanley Lord
First Officer
Second Officer

ON THE *OLYMPIC*
Captain
Fred Barrett

SCENE ONE

Narrator #1: It's Wednesday morning, April 17, 1912, in the Senate office building in Washington D.C. Maggie Molloy, an aide to Senator William Alden Smith, talks with a senate page.

Senate Page: I still don't believe the *Titanic* sank. It said in the newspapers that God Himself could not sink that ship!

Molloy: I don't want to believe it, either. But from the look on Senator Smith's face, the worst rumors must be true.

Narrator #2: A buzzer rings on Maggie's desk, summoning her into the senator's office. She enters to find Senator Smith sitting sadly behind his desk.

Smith: Maggie, did you get me a ticket on the next train to New York?

Molloy (*handing him a ticket*): Yes, sir. Here it is.

Smith: Thank you. The ship *Carpathia* is due in tonight. She carries the survivors from the *Titanic*. I want to be there when the ship docks.

Molloy: Are the rumors true, then? Did many people die when the *Titanic* sank?

Smith (*glumly*): I just got off the phone with the President. He told me that more than 1,500 people perished.

Molloy (*shocked*): How could such a tragedy happen?

Smith: That is what I'm going to find out.

SCENE TWO

Narrator #1: Smith arrives at the New York City docks just as the *Carpathia* pulls into the docks. It is a dark, cold night. A freezing drizzle falls on thousands of people crowding the docks. Many of them are friends or loved ones of people who set sail on the *Titanic*.

Narrator #2: Smith walks up the gangplank onto the Carpathia. He goes to the cabin where Bruce Ismay sits in darkness. Ismay, president of the company that owned the *Titanic*, survived the shipwreck.

Smith: Mr. Ismay, I am Senator William Alden Smith. I have the permission of the President and the United States Senate to investigate the sinking of the *Titanic*.

Ismay (*sighing*): I understand. And I'll do what I can to help. But you must understand, Senator Smith, that a tragedy of this size can only be an act of God.

Narrator: Later, Smith leaves the ship. He passes through the crowd of waiting people. Everyone in the crowd is crying. A few people weep with joy at the sight of their loved ones. Many more, though, wail with sadness.

SCENE THREE

Narrator #1: The next morning, Smith and a team of other senators begin hearings. The first witness is Bruce Ismay.

Smith: Mr. Ismay, tell us what you know about what happened to the *Titanic*.

Ismay: It was the ship's first voyage. We left Southampton, England, and made stops at Cherbourg, France, and Queenstown, Ireland. At about 11:40 Sunday night the *Titanic* struck an iceberg. The ship sank at 2:20. That, sir, I think is all I can tell you.

44

Smith: Why were you on the *Titanic*, Mr. Ismay?

Ismay: I always travel on our new ships. I like to see how they perform. And the *Titanic* was the finest ship ever built.

Smith: Were all of the women and children on board saved?

Ismay: I am afraid not, sir.

Smith: How many were saved?

Ismay: I have no idea. I have not asked. Since the accident I have made very few inquiries of any sort.

Smith: Hmmm. How is it, sir, that you made it to a lifeboat, when so many women and children did not?

Ismay (*blushing*): I was helping the sailors load the lifeboats. There were no more passengers on the deck, so I got in.

Smith: Could you describe how the ship sank?

Ismay: No, sir. I did not see the *Titanic* sink.

Smith (*surprised*): You didn't see it? How far away was your lifeboat?

Ismay: I do not know, sir. I kept my back to the ship as she sank.

Smith: You didn't care to see the *Titanic* go down?

Ismay (*snapping*): I am *glad* I did not see her sink!

SCENE FOUR

Narrator #2: Next, Smith and the other senators question the *Titanic*'s second officer, Charles Lightoller.

Smith: Officer Lightoller, you are the most senior officer to survive the sinking, correct?

Lightoller: That's right, sir. Captain Smith and First Officer Murdoch both went down with the ship.

Smith: Tell us what happened that night.

Lightoller: I was on watch in the ship's bridge from 6 to 10 p.m. That meant I was in charge of the ship. I'll always remember that night. The air was cold, and the ocean was as calm as a pond. Captain Smith stopped on the bridge before turning in for the night...

Flashback
On the *Titanic*, April 14, 9:10 p.m.

Narrator #1: Second Officer Lightoller and Captain Smith stand on the bridge of the *Titanic*, looking out over the water.

Captain Smith: It certainly is a clear night.

Lightoller: Yes, sir. And I've never seen the ocean this calm. It looks like a sheet of glass.

Captain Smith: We have received warnings from other ships in the area. There may be icebergs ahead.

Lightoller: I saw the warnings, sir. Should we slow down?

Captain Smith: Hmmm. Under these conditions, we should be able to see any ice far in advance. But if it gets at all hazy, then we should slow down.

Lightoller: Very good, sir.

Captain Smith: I'm off to my cabin, Lightoller. Let me know if the weather changes. (*smiles*) And try to keep warm, eh?

Lightoller: Aye-aye, sir.

Narrator #2: At 10 p.m., Lightoller's watch ends. He turns over command of the *Titanic* to First Officer William Murdoch.

Lightoller: Everything is under control, sir. Oh, yes. We've had ice warnings. We may be up around icebergs any time now.

Murdoch: On a night this clear, we should have no trouble seeing anything in our path. Good night, Lightoller. Get a good rest.

Lightoller: I hope to, sir.

Back at the Senate Hearing

Smith: So, as far as you know, the *Titanic* was going at top speed when she hit the iceberg?

Lightoller: I do not know, sir. I was off duty.

Smith: Well, who would know?

Lightoller: Captain Smith and First Officer Murdoch. (*grimly*) And you can't very well ask them, can you, sir?

SCENE FIVE

Narrator #1: The next witness is Frederick Fleet, a jumpy young man.

Smith: Relax, Mr. Fleet. We only want to learn the truth. You were in the crow's nest when the *Titanic* struck the iceberg, were you not?

Fleet: That's right, sir. I was on lookout with my mate, Reginald Lee. (*sadly*) Poor Reggie, he didn't make it.

Smith: Was there anything out of the ordinary on that night?

Fleet: Not really, sir. It was very calm and clear. And, golly, it was cold.

Smith: There was no moon, was there?

Fleet: No, sir. But the stars were bright. Still, if we only had a pair of binoculars....

Narrator: The crowd murmurs in surprise.

Smith: Wait a second, Mr. Fleet. Do you mean to say that there were no binoculars for the men on lookout?

Fleet: That's right, sir.

Smith: Why not?

Fleet (*shrugs*): You know how it is, sir. It was the ship's first voyage. Everyone was in a mad rush to get ready. Lots of little details were forgotten. (*sighs*) Still, I'll always wonder what might have happened if we had binoculars....

Flashback
On the *Titanic*, April 14, 11:39 p.m.

Narrator #2: Fleet and Reginald Lee huddle in the crow's nest. The cold night air whistles by them.

Fleet: Blimey, it's cold. And look at all those stars.

Lee: At least we're making good time.

Narrator #1: Fleet stares ahead. On the horizon, dead ahead of the ship, a tiny black mass blocks the stars.

Fleet: There's ice ahead!

Narrator #2: Fleet rings a warning bell three times, then grabs the telephone linking the crow's nest to the bridge. On the bridge, Officer James Moody picks up the phone.

Moody: What do you see?

Fleet: Iceberg right ahead, sir!

Moody: Thank you.

Narrator #1: Moody slams down the phone and turns to First Officer Murdoch.

Moody: Iceberg dead ahead, sir!

Narrator #2: Murdoch rushes to the controls and signals the engine room to reverse the engines. He turns to the helmsman.

Murdoch: Hard starboard!

Helmsman: Hard starboard, sir!

Narrator #1: The helmsman spins the wheel in a desperate attempt to steer the great ship around the iceberg. In the crow's nest, Fleet and Lee watch, terrified, as the iceberg looms larger and larger. Soon the giant mountain of ice towers over the bow of the ship.

Fleet: Come on. Turn. Turn!

Narrator #2: Then, at the last possible moment, the bow of the ship turns aside.

Lee: We're going to make it!

Narrator #1: The *Titanic* passes along the side of the iceberg. As it does, Fleet hears a grinding sound. Huge chunks of ice drop from the berg and crash onto the deck.

Narrator #2: Then, in less then ten seconds, the *Titanic* passes by the iceberg, which disappears behind it into the night. Fleet turns to Lee.

Fleet: Whew! That was a close shave!

Back at the Senate Hearing

Smith: How far was the *Titanic* from the iceberg when you first saw it?

Fleet: I'm not sure, sir. Maybe a mile. Probably less.

Smith: And if you had binoculars, could you have seen the iceberg sooner?

Fleet: A bit sooner, sir.

Smith: How much sooner?

Fleet (*quietly*): Soon enough to get out of the way.

SCENE SIX

Narrator #1: The next witness causes a stir in the Senate chambers. It's 22-year-old Harold Bride. He enters the room in a wheel chair, his left foot wrapped in a bandage.

Smith: What is wrong with your foot, young man?

Bride: Frostbite, sir. I was in the freezing water for quite a few hours.

Smith: You were one of the wireless telegraph operators on the *Titanic*, weren't you?

Bride: Yes, sir. She had the most powerful signal of any ship afloat.

Smith: Who did you report to? Captain Smith?

Bride: Actually, sir, we're employed by the telegraph company. I reported to Jack Phillips, the senior telegraph operator on the ship. Last Sunday, I came in to take over for Jack right at midnight....

Flashback
On the *Titanic*, April 14-15, midnight

Narrator #2: Harold Bride stifles a yawn as he enters the telegraph office, located just off the bridge. Jack Phillips hunches over the telegraph, working.

Bride: Are you caught up with the backlog of messages?

Phillips: Not even close. You'll be busy all night long, my friend.

Narrator #1: Bride hears officers yelling commands on the bridge.

Bride: What's going on?

Phillips: I'm not sure. I think we may have hit something a few minutes ago. I wouldn't be surprised if the ship had to go in for some repairs once we get back to England.

Narrator #2: The door opens. Captain Smith, his face pale, sticks his head in.

Captain Smith: You had better get assistance!

Phillips: What's that, sir? You want me to send out a distress signal?

Captain Smith: Yes. Right away!

Narrator #1: Smith drops the message he has been sending and immediately sends a distress call.

Bride: What signal are you sending?

Phillips: The standard message—CQD.

Bride: Send SOS. It's the new distress call, and it may be your last chance to send it.

Narrator #2: Phillips sends out the SOS signal to all ships within range of his radio. Outside, Bride hears crewmen calling orders back and forth. He looks out the door.

Bride: Blimey. This must be serious. They're uncovering the lifeboats.

Phillips: Probably just a precaution.

Narrator #1: Soon Captain Smith returns to the telegraph office.

Captain Smith: Have you had any luck?

Phillips: The nearest ship to respond is the *Carpathia*, sir.

Captain Smith: How far away is she?

Phillips: She'll be here in about four hours.

Captain Smith (*muttering*): Too long...too long. (*to Phillips*) Keep trying!

Phillips: Yes, sir.

Back at the Senate Hearing

Smith: How long did Phillips keep sending the message?

Bride: Right up to the end, sir. We left the telegraph office when the water came washing in the door.

SCENE SEVEN

Narrator #2: After days of hearings in New York, Senator Smith and the other senators decide to take a brief break. They agree to resume their hearings in Washington, D.C. on April 21. When he returns to Washington, Senator Smith meets his aide Maggie Molloy.

Molloy: Welcome back, Senator.

Smith: What is in all of these bags stacked in my office?

Molloy: Mail, sir. People all around the country are writing to say that you're doing a great thing in the *Titanic* hearings.

Smith: That's good to hear.

Molloy: You've received some messages that are not so encouraging. For example, the British Ambassador has threatened to lodge a formal complaint.

Smith: Why?

Molloy: The *Titanic* was a British ship, with a British crew. The ambassador wonders why Americans are conducting an investigation.

Smith: Because Americans died on that ship! And hundreds of people who dreamed of becoming Americans, people who had scraped together the money to immigrate to our country died, too. (*grimly*) I will not give up. The surface has barely been scratched. The real investigation is yet to come.

SCENE EIGHT

Narrator #1: The senate hearings resume. The next witness is Fourth Officer Joseph Boxhall.

Smith: Officer Boxhall, what were your duties on the *Titanic*?

Boxhall: I was the ship's navigator, sir.

Smith: You kept track of the ship's position?

Boxhall: Yes, sir. I also plotted the position of icebergs as they were reported by other ships.

Smith: Had the *Titanic* received many warnings of icebergs?

Boxhall: Yes, sir.

Narrator #2: The crowd murmurs at this.

Smith: Tell us what happened that night.

Boxhall: Shortly after we hit the iceberg, I joined Captain Smith on the bridge....

Flashback
On the *Titanic*, April 14, 11:45 p.m.

Narrator #1: Captain Smith and Fourth Officer Boxhall face First Officer Murdoch.

Captain Smith: What happened, Murdoch?

Murdoch: We saw an iceberg dead ahead of the ship, sir. I gave orders to steer clear of it. I'm afraid she brushed the side of the ship.

Captain Smith (*to Boxhall*): Go below decks to assess the damage.

Boxhall: Aye-aye!

Captain Smith: Someone go find Mr. Andrews!

Narrator #2: Boxhall rushes to the bow of the ship. He sees dozens of passengers having a snowball fight with ice from the iceberg.

Boxhall (*to himself*): I hope that's the worst of the ice!

Narrator #1: Boxhall heads down a staircase into the bowels of the ship. Near the keel of the ship, he sees two seamen struggling up the stairs. They haul soaking wet bags of mail.

Boxhall: What's the story below?

Seaman #1: The mail room is flooding fast!

Boxhall: Is that the only place taking on water?

Seaman #2: No, sir! There's water coming in as far back as Boiler Room 5!

Narrator #2: Boxhall rushes back to the bridge with the news. He finds Captain Smith huddled over blueprints of the ship. Alongside him is Thomas Andrews, the man who designed the *Titanic*.

Boxhall: Sir, we have water leaking into the ship from the bow to Boiler Room 5.

Andrews: I was afraid of that.

Captain Smith: Is it bad, Mr. Andrews?

Andrews: It is fatal, Captain. The ship's first five watertight compartments have been damaged. Once they fill with water, the ship will tip forward. Then the other compartments will start to fill. Soon the entire ship will be dragged under.

Narrator #1: A grim silence falls on the men.

Captain Smith: Mr. Murdoch, please prepare the lifeboats. Begin to load the passengers. I will tell the radio operators to send a distress signal.

Murdoch: The lifeboats, Captain? But there are more than 2,000 people on board. There is space for less than half that number on the lifeboats.

Captain Smith (*quietly*): I am aware of that, Mr. Murdoch. Kindly do your duty.

Back at the Senate Hearing

Smith: So the "watertight" compartments were not watertight?

Boxhall: Not exactly, sir. They were not sealed on top, so water could spill over the top. But if the ship had only been damaged in the first three or four compartments, she would have survived.

Smith: But that was not what happened. Go on with your story.

Boxhall: Captain Smith sent me to wake up Second Officer Lightoller. He took charge of the lifeboats on one side of the ship. First Officer Murdoch took charge on the other side. I made my way back to the bridge. When I got there, Captain Smith was looking out over the water....

Flashback
On the *Titanic*, April 15, 12:05 a.m.

Narrator #2: Captain Smith peers at the horizon through a pair of binoculars.

Captain Smith: Mr. Boxhall, what do you see in the distance?

Boxhall: It looks like.... It is! It's a ship!

Captain Smith: That's what I thought. Go to the lamp and signal a distress call!

Narrator #1: Boxhall goes to a powerful electric lamp and begins flashing Morse code to the distant ship.

Boxhall (*anxious*): Why don't they reply?

Captain Smith: Fire the rockets. Send one up every five minutes until you have launched them all.

Back at the Senate Hearing

Narrator #2: The crowd buzzes at Boxhall's story.

Smith: There was another ship within sight of the *Titanic*? That's incredible!

Boxhall: I saw it with my own eyes. So did Captain Smith.

Smith: Why didn't they come to your rescue?

Boxhall (*sadly*): I wish I knew, sir. I wish I knew.

SCENE NINE

Narrator #1: The next star witness is Fifth Officer Harold Lowe.

Smith: Mr. Lowe, you claim that you were asleep in your bunk when the *Titanic* struck the iceberg.

Lowe: Yes I was, sir. You must remember that when we are at sea, we do not have too much time to sleep. And therefore when we sleep, we die.

Smith: What happened that night?

Lowe: I was woken up by voices. I looked out and saw passengers walking through the passageway. They all wore their life-belts. I went back into my bunk, threw on my clothes and got my revolver.

Smith (*surprised*): What for?

Lowe: Well, sir, you never know when you'll need it. I made my way up to the bridge....

Flashback
On the *Titanic*, April 15, 12:30 a.m.

Narrator #2: Lowe comes to the bridge.

Lowe: What's going on?

Boxhall: We hit an iceberg! Go help load the lifeboats.

Narrator #1: Lowe helps load the lifeboats on the starboard side of the ship. The deck is filling up with passengers, all wearing life vests. They shiver in the icy cold air. Some passengers are still in their pajamas and robes. All of them are confused.

Female Passenger: This is an outrage, waking us from our beds like this! I shall complain to the owners of this ship.

Ismay: Ma'am, please get in the lifeboat. You must hurry!

Narrator #2: Ismay helps the crew to load the lifeboats. When one of the boats is about half full, he turns to the crew members manning the ropes.

Ismay: What are you waiting for? Lower the boat!

Lowe: We will, if you get out of the way, you fool!

Seaman #3: Blimey, do you know who you just yelled at? That's Mr. Ismay. He owns this ship!

Lowe: Yes? Well, he can have it. It won't be worth much a few hours from now.

Narrator #1: As the *Titanic*'s bow settles lower and lower in the water, people grow more frightened. One man, Benjamin Hart, places his wife, Esther, and young daughter, Eva, on a lifeboat.

Esther Hart: We hate to leave you behind.

Benjamin Hart: Don't worry, my dear. I'm sure there's nothing to worry about. You'll be back on board for breakfast.

Narrator #2: At that moment, the first rocket shoots off from the ship's bridge and explodes over the *Titanic*. It sends a shower of white sparks onto the water.

Eva Hart: It's so pretty!

Narrator #1: Esther Hart gives a frightened look to her husband. He kisses her on the cheek.

Benjamin Hart: Good-bye, my dear.

Narrator #2: He watches sadly as the half-empty boat is lowered to the ocean.

Back at the Senate Hearing

Smith: Mr. Lowe, why is that so many of the lifeboats were lowered half-empty?

Lowe: Well, sir, they were designed to hold 65 people...in the water. But some of the officers were afraid that if we packed the lifeboats full, then they would collapse before they ever got in the water.

Smith: But didn't you conduct tests before setting sail? And once at sea, didn't you have lifeboat drills?

Lowe: I believe there was one scheduled for that Sunday morning, sir. Captain Smith canceled it.

Smith: Why did he do that?

Lowe: He wanted to attend Sunday church services, sir.

SCENE TEN

Narrator #1: A friend of Senator Smith's, an older man named Archibald Gracie, survived the wreck of the *Titanic*. He came before Senator Smith and the other senators.

Gracie: By two o'clock in the morning, it was apparent to everyone that the *Titanic* would sink. By that time, all of the standard lifeboats had been launched....

Flashback

On the *Titanic*,
April 15, 2:05 a.m.

Narrator #2: Gracie stands with a group of men on the top deck of the *Titanic*. Two of the men wear tuxedoes. Gracie smiles at them.

Gracie: Got dressed for the occasion, did you?

Man in Tuxedo: If we are to go down, at least we will go down like gentlemen.

Seaman #4: Look! There are two more lifeboats stowed on the roof of the officer's cabin!

Lightoller: We forgot about those. Give me a hand!

Narrator #1: Gracie climbs onto the roof of the cabin and helps Lightoller and the other seamen with the two spare lifeboats.

Seaman #4: Darn it, I can't get this rope untied.

Gracie: Cut the rope! Here, use my pen-knife. I can't believe that there are no tools here to help free the boats.

Narrator #2: At that instant, the *Titanic* lurches forward in the water. The bow sinks lower and lower, as its stern begins to rise out of the water. Hundreds of screaming people rush up from below deck. They head for the ship's rising stern.

Gracie (*upset*): Look at all of those women and children. I thought they had all left the ship by now! (*calls to a passing woman*) Why didn't you leave on a lifeboat?

Woman: We were down below in the third-class lounge, sir. We didn't know what was going on!

Narrator #1: The *Titanic* lunges deeper into the water. A huge wave rolls up the deck. Lightoller dives off the roof and into the onrushing water. Gracie grabs hold of the ship's rail and is dragged under the water.

Narrator #2: With an echoing roar, one of the giant smokestack funnels explodes off the ship, crashing into the water. It crushes dozens of people struggling in the water.

Narrator #1: The great ship seems to do a headstand in the water. The bow disappears under the surface, while the stern rises straight up.

Narrator #2: On board, hundreds of screaming people cling to the rails and try climbing to the stern of the boat. Somehow, the lights of the ship still burn. Then, with a flash, the lights go off.

Narrator #1: With a series of thundering "booms," the Titanic breaks in two. Its bow, filled with water, plunges into the deep. The stern settles back into the water, then raises straight out of the water.

Narrator #2: It stays there for minutes, with hundreds of screaming people hanging on for dear life. Then the stern slowly, silently, slides under the water.

Back at the Senate Hearing

Smith: How did you survive the shipwreck, Mr. Gracie?

Gracie: As the *Titanic* plunged under water, I let go of the railing and swam for the surface. When I finally made it, I saw the spare lifeboat we had struggled to get off the roof. It had slipped free of the ship, and was now floating upside down. I climbed onto the boat, joining Lightoller and a dozen other men already there. It is a miracle I escaped death.

Smith: Were there many others left in the water?

Gracie: Of course there were. Hundreds of poor souls, screaming for help, as they slowly froze to death. (*shudders*) I shall never forget the sound of their cries.

SCENE ELEVEN

Narrator #1: Senator Smith meets with Maggie Molloy.

Molloy: Senator, have you seen these newspapers from England? They all claim that your are insensitive and acting like a fool. They call for the British government to insist that you let the British sailors and officers return home.

Smith: I am sorry if my questions hurt any feelings. But I would rather hurt their feelings than to see more people suffer as the people on the *Titanic* suffered!

Narrator #2: Back at the hearings, Senator Smith questions Third Officer Herbert Pitman.

Smith: Mr. Pitman, you were in charge of one of the lifeboats. Describe what happened after the *Titanic* sank.

Pitman: It was awful. All of the people in the water were crying, shouting, moaning.

Smith: What did you do?

Flashback
In the Lifeboats, April 15, 2:30 a.m.

Narrator #1: Pitman commands a half-empty lifeboat. It is lashed to another half-empty lifeboat. They are a few hundred yards from where the *Titanic*

sank. The water is covered with people screaming for help.

Pitman: Now, men, let's row back toward the wreck. We can pick up some more survivors.

First Man: Are you mad? They will swamp the boat. We'll all die!

Pitman: But there are only 40 of us in the two boats. We have room for at least 60 more.

Second Man: I say, if we go back there we won't save 60 people. We will only add 40 names to the list of those who drowned.

Seaman #5: Well sir, should we row back there, or not?

Narrator: Pitman is torn.

Back at the Senate Hearing

Narrator #2: The room is hushed. Senator Smith stares at Pitman.

Smith: You did not go back to save any others, did you?

Pitman (*quietly*): No, sir. We did not go back to save anyone. None of the lifeboats did.

SCENE TWELVE

Narrator #1: Senator Smith again talks to Maggie Molloy.

Smith: There's one thing about this tragedy that bothers me more than anything else.

Molloy: What's that?

Smith: The so-called "mystery ship." Officer Boxhall says that he and Captain Smith both saw the lights of a ship near the *Titanic*. If there really was another ship close by, then everyone on board could have been saved.

Molloy: Yes, but no other ships report being near the *Titanic*.

Narrator #2: A senate page bursts into the office.

Senate Page: Senator Smith! Have you seen the newspapers? A sailor from a ship called the *Californian* has come forward. He claims that they were within ten miles of the Titanic as she sank...and that their captain did nothing!

Smith: Well, well, well. We'll have to have a talk with that captain.

Narrator #1: Within days, the captain of the *Californian*, Stanley Lord, comes before the Senate Committee.

Smith: Captain, please tell us what happened on the night of Sunday, April 14.

Lord: Certainly. Our ship had steamed along all day and encountered ice on more than one occasion. We sent out warning to all ships in the area...including the *Titanic*. By 10:30 I ordered us to stop for the night....

Flashback
On the *Californian*, April 14, 11:50 p.m.

Narrator #2: Captain Lord stands on the bridge of his ship, watching the horizon to the south. Two of his officers are there, too.

Lord: How long ago did you first see the lights of that ship?

First Officer: Twenty minutes ago, sir. Ten minutes ago the lights disappeared, as though the ship had turned sharply. Then they stopped dead in the water.

Lord: It doesn't look like a passenger ship.

First Officer: It is, sir.

Lord: Hmmm. Well, try to signal it with our Morse lamp.

Narrator #1: Lord retired to his cabin. After an hour and a half, he called up to the bridge through his speaking tube.

Lord: Is that ship still there?

First Officer: Yes, sir. But it's not coming any nearer.

Lord: Whoever it is has the good sense to stop due to the ice. (*yawning*) I'm going to turn in.

First Officer: Sir...that ship has sent up rockets.

Lord: Well, keep sending the Morse signal.

Narrator #2: Lord curls up in his bunk and falls asleep. On the bridge, his officers continue to watch the strange lights.

First Officer: There goes another rocket!

Second Officer: And those lights look queer...hold on. They're gone. The ship has disappeared.

First Officer: I had better go tell the captain.

Narrator #1: The First Officer enters Captain Lord's cabin.

First Officer: Sir, that ship has disappeared. Before it went, it launched eight rockets.

Lord (*half-asleep*): All right. (*yawns*) What time is it?

Back at the Senate Hearing

Lord: It was 2:30 in the morning.

Smith: Captain Lord, you admit that you saw another ship. And you saw that ship firing rockets.

Lord: Yes, sir. But, according to my calculations, we were at least 19 miles from the *Titanic*. There was no way we could have seen her from that distance.

Smith: Is it possible that you were closer than that?

Lord (*stiffly*): Not according to my calculations. There must have been another ship that came between us. That's the ship that Captain Smith saw, and that's the ship that I saw.

Smith: The facts remains. You saw another ship. You saw it fire rockets. And yet, you never even bothered to have your wireless operator turn on his radio to check for distress calls!

Lord: No, sir. And when we did turn on our radio the next morning and I heard the news about *Titanic*...I was shocked, sir. Shocked.

SCENE THIRTEEN

Narrator #2: The Senate hearing winds down. Senator Smith decides to call one last witness for a second time— Bruce Ismay.

Smith: Mr. Ismay, one question haunts me. Why was the *Titanic* going so fast despite the ice warnings?

Ismay: You would have to ask Captain Smith that.

Smith: You didn't order the captain to go at top speed in order to impress the public, did you?

Ismay: Never, sir.

Smith: You did not, at any time, urge the captain to greater speed?

Ismay: No, sir. No one on the ship could do that. Captain Smith was in complete charge. But I can tell you this—the *Titanic* was not going at top speed that night.

SCENE FOURTEEN

Narrator #1: The Senate concludes its hearing and begin preparing a report. Senator Smith sees in the newspaper that the *Olympic*, the sister ship to the *Titanic*, has docked in New York.

Narrator #2: Smith decides to visit the ship, which is the same size as the *Titanic*. The captain of the *Olympic* greets Senator Smith on the deck.

Smith (*looking around*): I'm glad to see you carry more lifeboats than the *Titanic* had.

Captain: Yes, sir. We added them after the accident. Now there's enough room for every man, woman, and child on the ship.

Smith: Could you show me how they work?

Captain: Certainly.

Narrator #1: The captain orders six of his crewmen to prepare a lifeboat. They have it ready in minutes.

Smith: Do you mind loading it with people before you launch it?

Captain: Whatever you say, sir.

Narrator #2: Smith watches as 65 sailors climb onboard the lifeboat. It is easily lowered to the water.

Smith: Amazing, what a crew can do...when they are trained.

Captain: You know, Senator, we have a survivor from the *Titanic* working in our boiler room.

Smith: Really? I'd love to meet him.

Captain: I'll send for him.

Smith: No, no. I'll go visit him in the boiler room.

Narrator #1: Senator Smith descends into the hot, steamy bowels of the ship. He meets Fred Barrett, a wiry man, who shovels coal into the great boilers.

Barrett: I was working that night in *Titanic*'s Boiler Room 5. I reckon I was the first man to know that the *Titanic* had struck the berg. The water came spraying in like it was shot from a fire hose.

Smith: You were working hard that night?

Barrett: Of course. You see that white signal light over there? It means " full speed ahead." That light was a-blazing when we hit the ice.

Smith: Really?

Barrett: Yes. That very day, we lit up three of the boilers for the first time.

Smith: So...the *Titanic* was going full speed, after all.

Barrett: As fast as she would ever go, guv'nor. She was going as fast as she would ever go.

SCENE FIFTEEN

Narrator #2: Late one night, Senator Smith sits at his desk, writing. Maggie Molloy comes in.

Molloy: What are you working on so late at night, sir?

Smith: Tomorrow I make my speech to the Senate on the *Titanic*. I have much to say.

Molloy: Can we prevent other disasters like the *Titanic*?

Smith: I believe we can.

Molloy: How?

Smith: First, we must never blame the Almighty for our own mistakes.

EPILOGUE

In the months after the *Titanic* sank, the United States and other countries passed many laws in order to prevent another disaster like the wreck of the Titanic. Among the laws passed were:

All ocean liners must carry enough lifeboats for every man, woman, and child on board the ship.

All ships' telegraph radios must be working and manned 24 hours a day while at sea.

The passenger ship sea lanes in the North Atlantic were moved 60 miles to the south during the icy season.

Titanic Facts

It took three years to build the *Titanic*. The ship cost more than $10 million to build—a mind-boggling amount back in 1912.

From front to back the *Titanic* measured 882 feet. (That's almost as long as three football fields.) The ship displaced 66,000 tons of water. The steel plates of the *Titanic* were held in place by more than 3 million rivets. (The rivets alone weighed 1,200 tons.) The ship's mammoth rudder was as tall as a house, and weighed 100 tons. The *Titanic* had three giant propellers, powered by steam engines able to churn out power equal to the strength of 46,000 horses.

TITANIC COINCIDENCES

Novelist Morgan Robertson wrote a book titled *Futility* in 1898, 14 years before the *Titanic* sank. It told the story of a huge ocean liner filled with wealthy passengers. The ship had almost exactly the same dimensions as the *Titanic*.

In Robertson's story, the ship struck an iceberg one cold April night and sank in the Atlantic Ocean. Most of its 3,000 passengers and crew died because the ship did not have enough lifeboats.

The name of the ship in Robertson's novel was the *Titan*!

Robertson's book wasn't the only literary prediction of the *Titanic* disaster. Senator William Alden Smith carried a poem in his wallet. He clipped it from a newspaper more than ten years before the *Titanic* sank. It read:

> Then she, the stricken hull,
> the doomed, the beautiful,
> Proudly to fate abased,
> her brow... *Titanic*.

Senator Smith could never explain what impulse made him clip and save the poem.

TITANIC TREASURES

Perhaps the single most valuable object on board the *Titanic* was a jewel-encrusted copy of the *Rubaiyat of Omar Kayyam*, an ancient book. Also, the wealthy passengers in first class traveled with money and fine jewelry — most of which was lost with the ship.

Of course, the greatest treasure on board the *Titanic* was its passengers and crew. The loss of 1,500 lives was devastating to the United States and to the world.

The Deadly Toll

Of the 2,295 people who set sail on the *Titanic*, 1,589 lost their lives when the ship sank. The chart tells how many lives were lost and saved in each class. Use the information to complete the graph below. Then answer the questions.

First-Class Passengers	
Lost	130
Saved	199
Second-Class Passengers	
Lost	166
Saved	119
Third-Class Passengers	
Lost	536
Saved	174
Crew	
Lost	685
Saved	119

TITANIC—THE DEADLY TOLL

First Class	S	X X X X X X X X X X X X X X X X X X X X
	L	X X X X X X X X X X X X X
Second Class	S	
	L	
Third Class	S	
	L	
Crew	S	
	L	

Each X stands for 10 people. *Hint:* Round the numbers to the nearest 10 before completing the graph.

Fill in the blanks.

1. Which class had the fewest passengers? _____

2. In which class would you have had the best chance of surviving? _____

3. Which class of passenger had the worst chance of surviving? _____

4. Complete the sentence: "If you were a member of the crew, the chance that you would have died was about _____ times greater than the chance you would have survived."

Send an SOS

The *Titanic* telegraph operators used a new invention to send their messages: the radio. In those early days of radio, the technology was not sophisticated enough to send voice messages. Instead, radio operators sent telegraph messages using Morse code.

Morse code breaks down the alphabet into a series of dots and dashes. With the telegraph, a dot is a short, quick signal. A dash is a longer signal.

There are other ways to send messages using Morse code. For instance, the *Titanic* had "Morse lamps." Those were powerful spotlights that could flash messages to other ships miles away. A dot would be a quick flash of light. A dash would be a longer flash of light.

Here is the Morse code. Work with a friend. Write a message letter by letter in the space provided. Then translate each letter into Morse code. Use flashlights to send your messages over a distance.

Morse Code		Message:
A	• –	
B	– • • •	
C	– • – •	
D	– • •	
E	•	
F	• • – •	
G	– – •	
H	• • • •	
I	• •	
J	• – – –	
K	– • –	
L	• – • •	
M	– –	
N	– •	
O	– – –	
P	• – – •	
Q	– – • –	
R	• – •	
S	• • •	
T	–	
U	• • –	
V	• • • –	
W	• – –	
X	– • • –	
Y	– • – –	
Z	– – • •	

THIINK ABOUT IT
The old distress call was CQD. Right before the Titanic set sail, SOS became the new distress call for ships at sea. Why do you think the distress call was changed?

Disaster Lab: Sink the Ship

You can make a model to show how the *Titanic* sank. Here's how:

You'll Need

- two aluminum-foil muffin pans
- three brass paper fasteners
- coins or other small weights
- a pen
- a sink or basin of water

STEP 1
Make Your Model
Fix the two aluminum-foil muffin pans together to make one long pan. Lay them end to end, with the edges overlapping. Fasten them together by carefully poking the three paper fasteners through the overlapping edges and opening the brads.

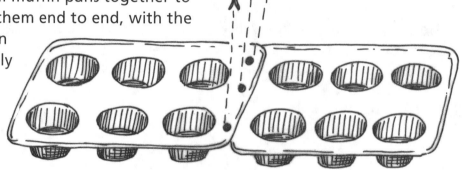

STEP 2
Float It and Load It
The muffin pans stand for the hull of the *Titanic*. The individual muffin holders are the watertight compartments. Place your model in a basin of water and observe how it floats. Next, stack coins or other weights on the edge of the pans. They stand for the ship's cargo and engines.

STEP 3
Sink the Ship
Using a pen, carefully poke large holes in the first two muffin holders. Observe what happens to the hull and to the cargo.

Poke holes in more of the muffin holders. Observe what happens to the hull and cargo.

How many of your "watertight compartments" can be damaged before your ship sinks?

The *Titanic* broke in two when it sank. What happens to your ship?

_____

_____

_____

Disasters Scholastic Professional Books

Earthquakes: Ready to Rumble

Background Information

Of all the disasters to strike humankind, earthquakes are perhaps the most destructive. To understand what causes earthquakes, your students must first understand some basic geology.

Use an orange or a hard-boiled egg to explain the earth's basic structure. Point out that the crust of the earth is like the shell of the egg or the peel on the orange. The crust is not intact, however. The cracks in the crust are called fault lines. Point out that fault lines are constantly grinding up against each other, and that energy builds up as the huge plates lock together. When they finally shift, the moving plates release great amounts of energy, causing earthquakes.

To demonstrate this concept, ask students to snap their fingers. Point out that the surfaces of their thumbs and fingers are like the edges of fault lines. Ask students to describe what they feel as they apply pressure between their thumbs and fingers (friction causes energy to build between the digits). What happened when the pressure becomes so great that the finger slips off the thumb? (The energy is released in the form of sound waves.) Ask students to imagine a similar buildup of energy, many billions times greater, between the different plates of the earth's crust along fault lines.

The following activities will help your students explore the causes and effects of earthquakes and how earthquakes are measured.

Earthquakes on a Plate

(Geography)

After students have read and completed the exercise on the Earthquakes on a Plate reproducible (page 64), discuss the following questions with the class:

1 How many earthquakes were on or near the coast of South America? (three)

2 How many earthquakes were on or near the coast of Asia? (two)

3 How many earthquakes were in the middle of a continent? (none)

4 Based on this map, how would you describe the relationship between earthquakes and fault lines? (Possible answer: Earthquakes almost always take place on or near fault lines.)

Disaster Lab: Tremors!

(Science)

Start the experiment by asking students what they think causes the destruction in earthquakes. Is it simply because earthquakes cause the ground to shake? Or do earthquakes cause waves to roll through the ground just as waves travel through water?

Preparation

Copy and distribute the Disaster Lab Sheet (page 65). Make available to students tablecloths or bedsheets made of thin fabric (paper is too stiff and might tear), along with decks of playing cards, building blocks, or other materials for building model buildings. Students can work in pairs or larger groups, depending on your classroom.

During the Activity

Have students follow the procedure on the lab sheets. Make sure that they make and record a hypothesis before they attempt the activity. As students do the activity, observe how they manipulate the sheet or tablecloth. Make sure that they do not tug or jerk the fabric violently. The point of the activity is to demonstrate how a disturbance in the earth's crust can cause destruction far away. Simply jerking the fabric to cause the buildings to collapse is not an accurate model of an earthquake.

Drawing Conclusions

Students should clearly understand that earthquakes are actually waves of energy moving through the earth's crust. You might use a basin of water and a marble to provide another model of the phenomenon. What happens when you drop the marble in the water? (Concentric waves ripple out from where the marble broke the surface of the water.) Ask students to imagine that the epicenter of an earthquake is like the marble breaking the surface of the water. The resulting waves are the earthquake tremors traveling through the earth's crust.

Magnitudes of Destruction: The Mercalli Scale and the Richter Scale

(Math, Language Arts)

Distribute both Magnitudes of Destruction: The Mercalli Scale (page 66) and Magnitudes of Destruction: The Richter Scale (page 67) to students. Allow students to read the information on the sheets. Point out that the Mercalli scale is older than the Richter scale. (The Mercalli scale was developed in 1902, the Richter scale in 1935.) Discuss the major differences between the two scales. Elicit from students that the Mercalli scale uses words to describe the power of an earth-

quake, while the Richter scale uses numbers. Ask: Which scale is easier to use? Which is more precise?

ANSWERS

Mercalli Scale	Richter Scale
1. V	1. 50,000
2. VII	2. 8,000
3. VIII, because that is the stage at which buildings are affected.	3. 100
	4. 50

How to Measure an Earthquake

(Math)

This reproducible (page 68) allows students to use the Richter scale to determine the power of earthquakes. Point out to students that the Richter scale uses data recorded on seismographs at a constant distance of 100 kilometers from the epicenter of an earthquake. Discuss why it is so important when measuring the power of earthquakes to always use data recorded at one set distance (By doing that, scientists are able to compare data from different earthquakes. If one earthquake was measured from 100 kilometers and another from 500, then the one measured from 100 kilometers might seem more powerful, even if it was not.)

ANSWERS

Earthquake A, 4.0

Earthquake B, 5.4

Earthquake C, 1.5

Earthquake D, 6.2

A Tale of Two Earthquakes

(Language Arts, Math)

On January 15, 1994, a major earthquake struck Los Angeles. Exactly one year later, another earthquake struck the Japanese port city of Kobe. Although the two earthquakes were close on the Richter scale, the Kobe earthquake was far more destructive.

Distribute the reproducible (page 69) and allow students to compare the data on the chart, then have them answer the questions. Ask students: Why was the Kobe earthquake so much more destructive? Remind students that the Richter scale is a logarithmic scale. That means that an earthquake registering 7 on the scale is ten times more powerful than one registering 6! Ask: What is the difference between the Kobe earthquake and the Northridge earthquake on the Richter scale? (6.9 - 6.7 = 0.2) How many more times powerful was the Kobe earthquake? (3 times more powerful)

ANSWERS

1. Kobe
2. Kobe
3. Possible answer: Since the Kobe earthquake took place more than an hour later, more people were out of bed and getting ready for the day or on their way to work, which put them more at risk
4. Possible answer: Kobe, since many more people were killed and injured in the earthquake.

For More on Earthquakes

Discovering Earthquakes by Nancy Field (Dog Eared Publishers, 1995). Features activities that explain earthquakes.

Earthquakes : Mind-Boggling Experiments You Can Turn Into Science Fair Projects by Janice VanCleave (John Wiley & Sons, 1993). A collection of 20 simple experiments that help students understand earthquakes.

Volcano & Earthquake by Susanna Van Rose (Knopf, 1992). Explores the causes and effects of volcanoes and earthquakes.

Earth: The Ever-Changing Planet by Donald Silver, illustrated by Patricia Wynne (Random House, 1989). Explains the natural forces that change and shape the earth. Covers earthquakes, plate tectonics, volcanoes, fossils, and more.

Fema for Kids (http://www.fema.gov/kids.htm). A Web site from the Federal Emergency Management Agency that includes information on earthquakes, hurricanes, floods, and other natural disasters, plus safety- and disaster-preparedness tips.

Earthquakes on a Plate

The earth is a giant ball made up of different layers.

Think of the earth as a giant egg. The crust is the shell of the egg. There are "cracks" on the shell. The map below shows them.

The sections of the earth's crust are called "tectonic plates." The lines where they meet are called "fault lines."

HOW EARTHQUAKES HAPPEN

The plates are constantly in motion. As the plates shift, friction traps energy along the fault lines. When that energy breaks free, the result is an earthquake.

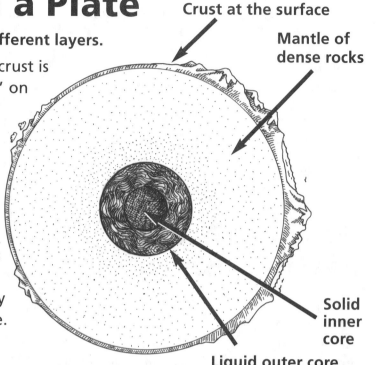

Crust at the surface

Mantle of dense rocks

Solid inner core

Liquid outer core

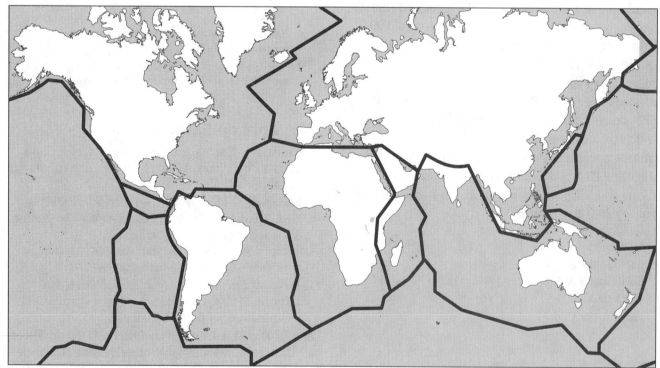

Here are the locations of recent earthquakes. Use an almanac or encyclopedia to mark them on the map above.

08/04/94 Near Coast of Ecuador	03/14/98 Northern Iran
07/17/98 New Guinea, Papua New Guinea	02/04/98 Afghanistan-Tajikistan Border
05/30/98 Afghanistan-Tajikistan Border	01/30/98 Northern Chile
05/22/98 Central Bolivia	01/14/98 Fiji Islands Region
05/03/98 Southeast of Taiwan	

Disaster Lab: Tremors!

What causes the most destruction in an earthquake, vibrations or waves? Do an experiment to find out.

What You'll Need

◈ A tablecloth or sheet (the thinner the fabric the better)

◈ A deck of playing cards or wooden blocks   ◈ A partner

STEP ONE: Are vibrations or waves more destructive in an earthquake? Record your hypothesis.

STEP TWO: Spread the tablecloth or sheet across the surface of a table.

◈ The fabric is the earth's crust.   ◈ The table is the earth's mantle.

Next, build card houses or houses from wooden blocks near one end of the sheet.

STEP THREE: Work with your partner. One of you is the "anchor." The anchor holds down the corners of the tablecloth nearest your buildings. The other one is the "tremor." The tremor goes to the the other end of the table and grasps the corners of the tablecloth and gently tugs the corners of the tablecloth in order to cause it to vibrate back and forth.

◈ What happens to the crust?   ◈ What happens to your buildings?

Carefully record your observations. Then "repair" any damaged buildings by rebuilding the card houses or restacking the wooden blocks.

STEP FOUR: Trade places with your partner. The "tremor" of the first experiment is now the "anchor," and vice versa. The tremor carefully lifts the far corners of the sheet about 18 inches off the table, then pulls them back down to the surface.

◈ What happens to the crust?   ◈ What happens to your buildings?

Record your observations.

STEP FIVE: Repeat the experiment at least two more times. Do your results change?

STEP SIX: Returns to your hypothesis. Did your experiment confirm your hypothesis? if necessary, rewrite your hypothesis to reflect your experiments.

Magnitudes of Destruction: The Mercalli Scale

There are two scales used to measure the strength, or *magnitude*, of an earthquake. The *Mercalli* scale describes the effects of an earthquake in a city or town. It uses Roman numerals so people won't confuse it with the Richter scale.

Intensity	Observed Effects
I	The earthquake is not felt. It is only sensed by seismographs.
II	Vibrations are felt only by a few people, usually those in upper floors of buildings.
III	Vibrations are felt by many people. Most who feel it are indoors, and may not know it is an earthquake. Lights and hanging plants swing.
IV	People indoors and outdoors feel the earthquake. Windows rattle. Parked cars rock back and forth.
V	The earthquake wakes up sleeping people. Small objects fall off shelves. Drinks spill.
VI	The earthquake is felt by everyone. Many people are frightened and run outdoors. Furniture may move.
VII	Vibrations make it difficult to stand. Furniture breaks. The earthquake causes waves in ponds and swimming pools.
VIII	Some houses may shift off of their foundations. Chimneys and towers may collapse.
IX	General panic strikes. The ground cracks. Underground pipes break. Some buildings collapse.
X	Many buildings collapse or are severely damaged. Bridges are destroyed.
XI–XII	Nearly total destruction.

1. You are fast asleep when a rumbling wakes you up. Books fall from your bookshelf. It's an earthquake! What is the Mercalli intensity of the quake?

   _____

2. You are standing by a pool, when a tremor knocks you off your feet. Water from the pool splashes over its edge. What is the Mercalli intensity of the earthquake?

   _____

3. In which number on the scale would you say an earthquake becomes dangerous?

   Explain. _____

   _____

   _____

   _____

   _____

   _____

   _____

Magnitudes of Destruction: The Richter Scale

There are two scales used to measure the strength, or *magnitude*, of an earthquake.

The *Richter* scale uses numbers to measure the waves caused by an earthquake. The scale is a logarithm. This means that each unit is ten times more powerful than the unit that came before. Scientists use decimals to show degrees between the numbers on the scale. For example, an earthquake reading 6.5 on the Richter scale would come halfway between 6 and 7 on the scale.

Richter Scale	Times Greater than 1
1	1
2	10
3	100
4	1,000
5	10,000
6	100,000
7	1,000,000
8	10,000,000
9	100,000,000

Use the scale above to answer the following questions.

1. How many more times powerful than 1 is an earthquake measuring 5.5?

_____

2. How many more times powerful than 1 is an earthquake measuring 4.8?

_____

3. How many more times powerful than 5 is an earthquake measuring 7?

_____

4. How many more times powerful than 2 is an earthquake measuring 3.5?

_____

Name _____   Date _____

How to Measure an Earthquake

Scientists use machines called seismographs to measure earthquakes. Seismographs record and provide data as earthquakes strike. That data is shown on a reading called a *seismogram*.

Here is a sample seismogram reading of an earthquake:

P-waves — Primary waves, or the first tremors of an earthquake.

S-waves — Secondary waves, which strike after Primary waves.

Amplitude — A measurement to reflect the power of a tremor.

Once scientists have collected data from a seismogram, they use the Richter scale to determine the strength of the earthquake.

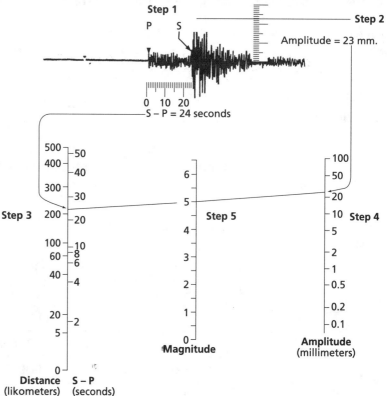

STEP 1: First, measure the amount of time from the first P-wave to the first S-wave. In this case, the S - P distance is 24 seconds.

STEP 2: Next, measure the wave with the greatest amplitude. In this case, the greatest amplitude is 23 mm.

STEP 3: Then use the scale to find the magnitude of the earthquake.

◈ Find the S - P distance on the left scale.

◈ Find the amplitude on the right scale.

◈ Use a ruler to connect the S - P distance and the amplitude. The point where the ruler crosses the middle scale is the magnitude.

In this case, the earthquake is 5.0 on the Richter scale.

Use the scale to determine magnitude of earthquakes with these measurements:

Earthquake A
S - P Distance: 14 seconds
Amplitude: 5 mm
Magnitude: _____

Earthquake B
S - P Distance: 32 seconds
Amplitude: 32 mm
Magnitude: _____

Earthquake C
S - P Distance: 2 seconds
Amplitude: 1 mm
Magnitude: _____

Earthquake D
S - P Distance: 45 seconds
Amplitude: 50 mm
Magnitude: _____

Disasters Scholastic Professional Books

A Tale of Two Earthquakes

One moment, everything is peaceful. The next moment, the ground itself heaves. Buildings fall down. Fires burst out. Bridges collapse. Roads cave in. Earthquakes are a constant threat in our world. Here are the facts about two recent deadly earthquakes:

	Northridge/Los Angeles, California	Kobe, Japan
Date	1/17/94	1/17/95
Time	4:30 a.m.	5:46 a.m.
Magnitude (Richter scale)	6.7	6.9
Deaths	57	4,569
Injured	about 9,000	14,679
Buildings Seriously Damaged	about 1,600	74,386

How often do earthquakes this powerful take place? An average of 120 earthquakes that measure between between 6.0 and 6.9 on the Richter scale strike the earth each year!

Questions:

1. Which city suffered a more powerful earthquake? _____

2. Which earthquake was more destructive? _____

3. How might the time at which each earthquake struck have affected the destruction it caused? Explain.

   _____

   _____

4. Based on this information, which city would you say is more densely populated, Kobe or Los Angeles? Explain.

   _____

   _____

   _____

5. If 120 earthquakes this severe happen each year, why are more cities not destroyed? Explain.

   _____

   _____

Hurricane!

Background Information

It is difficult to fathom the awesome power of a hurricane. These terrifying storms, caused by warm ocean water and hot, humid air in the tropic zones, are actually giant thermal engines unleashing vast amounts of energy. According to one estimate, the heat energy released by a hurricane in a single day is equal to the energy released by the fusion of 400 hydrogen bombs!

Begin your exploration of hurricanes by pointing out their frequency. During the hurricane season, which lasts from June through November, an average of six storms will form in the Atlantic Ocean. (In the Pacific, where the storms are called typhoons or cyclones, the stormy season never ends!)

Next, explain to students that the south is the region in the United States that has the fastest-growing population. Point out that there are now more than 45 million people living along the southern U.S. coastline, an area which is prone to hurricanes, and that more people move there every day! Discuss how the growing population demands that the government continue to improve its ability to identify and track hurricanes in order to provide early warnings to people at risk.

Copy the six reproducible sheets in this section. The first, Here Comes Andrew, gives your students the chance to track a hurricane's journey across the Atlantic Ocean. The sheets How to Make A Hurricane and Eye of the Storm take students inside a hurricane to see its causes and effects. The two-part Disaster Lab provides a hands-on demonstration of the power of air pressure and instructions for making a homemade barometer.

Here Comes Andrew

(Geography)

Hand out the reproducible Here Comes Andrew (pages 74–75). Review with students the use of latitude (signified by lines running horizontally across the map) and longitude (shown by vertical lines).

As they complete the worksheet, tell students that although it is impossible to predict the path a hurricane will take, meteorologists are able to make educated guesses by tracking winds and atmospheric pressure.

Use a blank copy of the map to track hurricanes and other storms during the autumn months.

ANSWERS

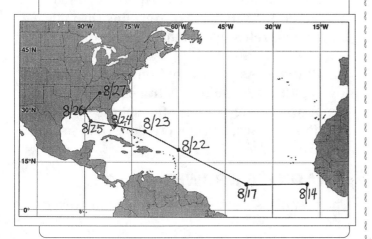

Inside a Hurricane

(Science)

Distribute the reproducibles How to Make a Hurricane and The Eye of the Storm (pages 76–78). Pose the following questions either as topics for discussion or for short written answers.

Discuss the following questions with students after they have read How to Make a Hurricane:

1 Why do hurricanes form in the tropics and not nearer to the poles? (Heat is needed to warm the water and air that fuel the storms.)

2 What happens to hurricanes once they come ashore? Why? (They lose their power, since they no longer are able to draw warm water from the ocean.)

3 What are the main differences between a Tropical Depression, Tropical Storm, and Hurricane? (The power of the wind grows stronger as a storm progresses from a Tropical Depression, to Tropical Storm, to Hurricane. Also, the circular motion of the storm grows more pronounced as it grows.)

4 What does the name "Tropical Depression" signify? (The term "depression" refers to the low-pressure area at the center of the storm.)

Discuss the following questions with students after they have read The Eye of the Storm:

1 What are the main destructive forces in a hurricane? Which one would you expect to be most destructive to buildings near the ocean's shore? (Storm surge; Wind; Rain; Possible answer: The storm surge would be most destructive near the shore, where it would cause floods.)

2 What part of the hurricane contains the strongest winds? (The eyewall)

3 A hurricane strikes. You weather the storm for hours. Then, suddenly, the wind dies. The rain stops, and the sun shines. Should you come out of hiding and begin cleaning up the damage? Explain. (No. You are in the eye of the hurricane. Once it passes, the storm will resume.)

4 Why do you think the National Hurricane Center is located in Miami? Explain. (Miami is near the Caribbean Sea. From there, it is easy for meteorologists to identify and track storms as they develop in the Atlantic Ocean.)

Hurricane Names

Language Arts

Hand out copies of the reproducible Hurricane Names (page 79) to the class. Explain that the World Meteorological Organization comes up with lists of names for hurricane and tropical storms. Each year they use a different list to name the hurricane and tropical storms for that year.

Next, as a class brainstorm a list of weather events that commonly occur in your part of the country (such as snowfalls, thunderstorms, wind storms). Your list doesn't have to be limited to storms. It could include days in which the temperature rises or falls below a certain level, sunny days, cloudy days, and so on.

List the different weather events on the chalkboard. Then divide the class into small groups and let each group select one of the weather events. Challenge each group to come up with a system for identifying the weather events as they occur over the course of the year, just as meteorologists track tropical storms and hurricanes by name. Remind students to keep the following points in mind:

◈ How will your naming system make it easy to keep track of the order of events? (For instance, hurricanes are named in alphabetical order.)

◈ Is your system open-ended? Does it need to be? (The naming system for hurricanes is closed, and allows for only 21 storms. In an average year, only six hurricanes strike, so the system does not need to be open-ended.)

Prepare a bulletin board where students can record weather events using their system over the course of the year.

Disaster Lab: Pressure Drop!

Science

Start the exploration of air pressure by asking students if they know how much air weighs.

Some students may argue that air doesn't have any weight since it is invisible. Point out that air is a medium we live in. Ask: Would a fish think that water has any weight? No, but we know that it does.

Make sure students understand that the earth's atmosphere is made up of gases. This blanket of gases has a weight that changes according to a variety of factors, such as altitude and weather systems. The relative "weight" of the air is measured and expressed in terms of air pressure.

Ask if any students have experienced pain in their ears when flying or traveling through mountains. Tell students that the discomfort is a result of different air pressures at different altitudes. As you travel from a higher to lower altitude, you literally travel into a region with more air. The atmosphere's weight increases, causing pressure (and pain) in the eardrum.

PART ONE: AIR POWER

The first disaster lab demonstrates the power of air pressure.

Preparation

Divide the class into small groups. Each group will need copies of Disaster Lab: Pressure Drop! (page 80), a glass bottle, a large bowl, and a small balloon. (Students will need access to a sink with hot and cold water.)

During the Activity

Make sure students do not overfill their bowls with cold water. They should leave enough room to submerge the bottle up to its neck without spilling water.

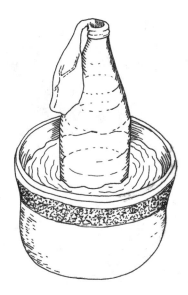

Drawing Conclusions

Discuss with students what made the balloon inflate inside the bottle. Point out that the lower air pressure inside the bottle literally meant that the "heavier" air outside the bottle moved in to inflate the balloon. Point out to students that their demonstration showed the power of air pressure on tiny scale. Challenge them to imagine how the violent changes in air pressure affect the power of a hurricane, a storm that towers 50,000 feet into the air and extends 500 miles across.

PART TWO: MAKE A BAROMETER

In this lab, students make a barometer—a tool for measuring air pressure.

Preparation

Have students work in small groups. Each group will need a copy of the reproducible Disaster Lab: Pressure Drop! (page 80), a glass or jar, a straw from a broom, index card, rubber band, and tape. Encourage each group to divide up the tasks, so that each member is responsible for one part of the experiment.

During the Activity

Students should make sure the plastic wrap is pulled taut over the top of the glass. They will only need tiny bits of tape to secure the broom straw. As they set up their barometers, instruct students to avoid placing them near windows or heating ducts, as their barometers will also be sensitive to temperature as well as air pressure.

Drawing Conclusions

After recording results over the course of two or three days, ask for a volunteer to describe the correlation between the weather and the position of the broom straw. In general, fair weather means higher air pressure. This causes the plastic wrap to cave in, which raises the straw. Rainy weather is usually accompanied by a low air-pressure system, which puffs up the plastic wrap, causing the straw to drop.

For More on Hurricanes

Hurricanes & Tornadoes by Neil Morris (Crabtree Publishing, 1998). From the "Wonders of Our World" series, this book explores these powerful storms. With information on predicting and preparing for them as well.

Hurricanes by Susan Hood (Simon Spotlight, 1998). Part of a series from the Weather Channel, filled with storms facts, trivia, and more.

Hurricanes: Earth's Mightiest Storms by Patricia Lauber (Scholastic, 1996). Introduce students to these powerful storms with full-color photographs, dramatic accounts of the 1938 hurricane in New England, Hurricane Andrew, and more.

Track current storms, look at satellite images of storms, and find information on the latest weather conditions on the National Oceanic and Atmospheric Administration's Web site (http://hurricanes.noaa.gov/).

Here Comes Andrew, Part 1

In August, 1992, Hurricane Andrew smashed into Florida and Louisiana. When it was over, the storm had wreaked more damage than any other hurricane in United States history. Andrew destroyed $25 billion worth of property, killed 40 people, and forced another 250,000 people to leave their homes.

To track Andrew: Put a dot on the place where the degrees of latitude and longitude intersect. When you are done, draw lines to connect the dots.

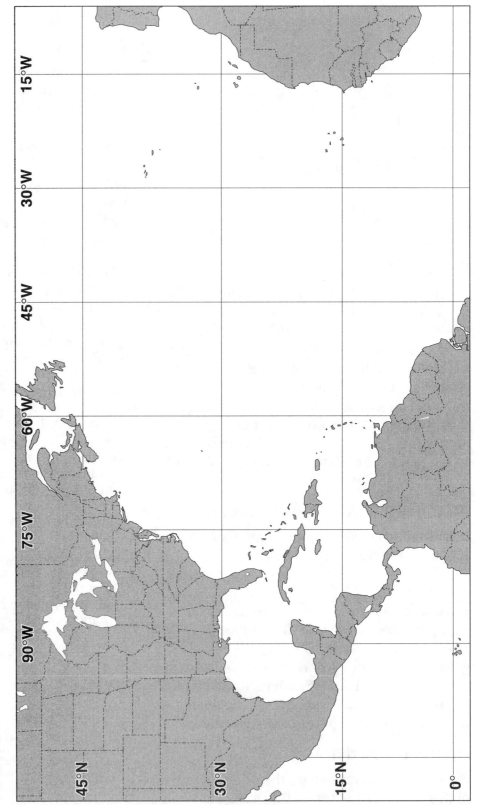

Here Comes Andrew, Part 2

Here's a day-by-day account of Andrew's progress. Track the storm on the map as it crosses the Atlantic Ocean.

Friday, August 14
20°W; 10°N

A patch of thunderstorms develop over western Africa. The storm system moves out over the warm, humid Atlantic Ocean.

Monday, August 17
40°W; 10°N

The storm system has turned a tropical storm. The World Meteorological Association names it "Andrew," since it is the Atlantic's first tropical storm of the season. The storm heads northwest.

Saturday, August 22
60°W; 20°N

Andrew's winds reach 74 miles per hour, and the storm is upgraded to a hurricane.

Sunday, August 23
70°W; 25°N

Andrew races across the Bahamas, causing terrible damage. The storm heads due west, and Florida braces for the worst.

Monday, August 24
81°W; 26°N

Andrew slams across Florida. With winds of at least 175 miles per hour, the storm destroys everything in its path. More than 80,000 dwellings are demolished, and another 55,000 are damaged.

Tuesday, August 25
86°W; 26°N

Andrew heads out over the Gulf of Mexico, where it gathers strength and turns to the northwest.

Wednesday, August 26
90°W; 30°N

Andrew comes ashore in rural Louisiana, rocking the coast with rain and high winds. Fifteen people are killed.

Thursday, August 27
85°W; 35°N

Andrew at last dies away, but not before pelting Mississippi, Alabama and Georgia with severe thunderstorms and high winds.

How to Make a Hurricane, Part 1

STAGES OF THE STORM

Meteorologists track three different stages in which a group of storms may grow into a full-fledged hurricane.

STAGE ONE: Tropical Depression

No, "tropical depression" is not how you feel when your Caribbean vacation comes to an end! It's actually a dangerous weather condition that is the first step toward a hurricane.

The "depression" is an area of low air pressure at the center of a weak storm system. The storms cluster around the pocket of low air pressure. At the surface of the water, the air begins to revolve around the pocket of low pressure. This pocket could become the eye of a hurricane.

A storm system is officially called a tropical depression when winds near the center blow 23 to 39 miles per hour.

STAGE TWO: Tropical Storm

When the winds in a tropical depression blow between 39 and 74 miles per hour, the weather system is upgraded to a "tropical storm." At this point, the storm is given an official name to help meteorologists track it. By now, the storm is definitely spinning counter-clockwise. Winds blow faster near the center of the storm than at the edge.

The harsh winds cause the warm ocean to become very turbulent. The high waves and choppy seas spew spray into the air. It evaporates, releasing even more moisture into the warm, wet air. This, in turn, fuels the growing storm.

The vicious circle is on its way to becoming a hurricane.

STAGE THREE: Hurricane

A giant circular windstorm with winds blowing at least 74 miles per hour is an official hurricane. The force of a hurricane can be 12,000 times greater than a normal storm. A typical hurricane towers 50,000 feet in the air and spans hundreds of miles. These giant storms cause terrible damage when they come ashore.

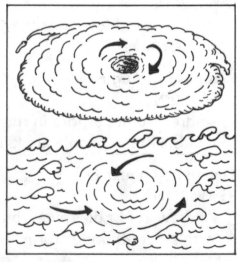

76

How to Make a Hurricane, Part 2

Ingredients

Here's what you need if you want to make a hurricane:

1. Warm ocean water

Waters in the tropic zones — the band of our planet near the equator — warm up during the summer months. These warm waters cause the air above them to grow hotter and more humid.

2. Hot, humid air

Hot, wet air hanging over the ocean rises far into the atmosphere. The humid air causes powerful thunderstorms to form.

3. Wind

Wind patterns can cause dozens of thunderstorms to cluster together. When a series of storms forms one huge storm...watch out! You might have a hurricane.

DID YOU KNOW?

In the eastern Pacific Ocean, hurricanes are known as typhoons. In the western Pacific and Indian Ocean, the storms are called cyclones.

Hurricanes spin counter-clockwise above the equator. Below the equator, the storms spin in a clockwise direction.

If the energy released by an average hurricane were converted to electricity, it would meet the United State's electrical needs for six months.

Through evaporation and sea spray, a typical hurricane can pick up 2 billion tons of ocean water each day.

WARNING! The Hurricane Warning Service carefully tracks all storms in the Atlantic Ocean. When storms threaten the coast, the National Hurricane Center, located in Miami, Florida, issues warnings. Here are the official warnings:

Tropical Storm Watch: Conditions are ripe for a tropical storm, with winds of 39 to 73 miles per hour.

Tropical Storm Warning: This warning is given when winds of 39 to 73 miles per hour are expected. The warning covers the area threatened by the storm. The chances are 1 in 3 that the center part of the warning area will be hit. There's a 1 in 4 chance that any location in the area will be hit by the storm.

Hurricane Watch: Hurricane conditions, with winds above 74 miles per hour, are a threat. In a hurricane watch, the odds are 1 in 3 that the center part of the area will be hit, and 1 in 4 that any part of the are will be hit.

Hurricane Warning: Watch out! A hurricane warning means that the chances are 1 in 2 that the center part of the warned area will be hit by a hurricane.

The Eye of the Storm

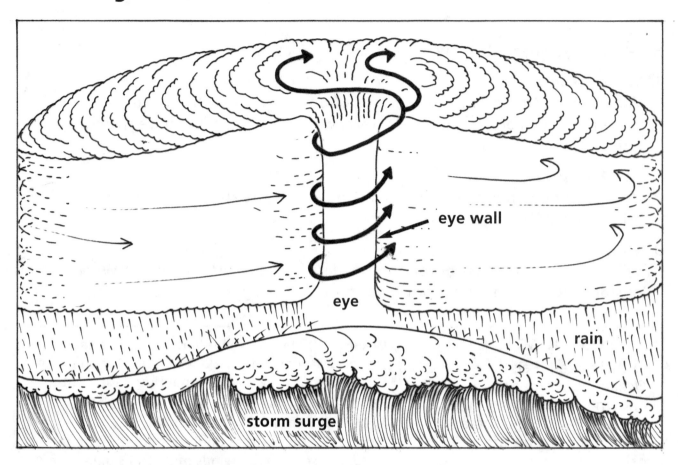

Here are the parts of a hurricane.

Eye: The calm center of the hurricane. It is a column of low air pressure 10 to 30 miles wide. When the eye of the hurricane passes, the rain can stop, winds calm down...the sun may even shine!

Eyewall: The part of the storm surrounding the eye is called the eyewall. The wind blows strongest here. It's the harshest, most turbulent part of the hurricane.

What makes hurricanes so deadly?

Storm Surge: Hurricane-force winds blow waves 60 feet high in the open ocean. Low air pressure causes the water to swell. When the storm hits land, a dome of water (called the storm surge) washes onshore. In a large hurricane, the storm surge can be 100 miles wide.

Wind: Hurricane-force winds can blow down buildings, uproot trees, roll cars, and send smaller items flying through the air like missiles.

Rain: During a hurricane, up to six inches of water can be dumped onto the ground within hours, causing deadly floods. For instance, in October 1998, thousands of people died in Central America after Hurricane Georges caused flooding and mudslides. The worst damage occurred hundreds of miles from the ocean.

Hurricane Names

The World Meteorological Organization comes up with the lists of names to give to hurricanes and tropical storms. The first storm of the season is given a name beginning with the letter A. The second storm is given name starting with B, and so on.

There are six lists. After six years, the first list is used over again. Sometimes, after a severe storm, the name is "retired" and replaced with a new name.

Did your name make it to one of the lists?

2000 Alberto, Beryl, Chris, Debby, Ernesto, Florence, Gordon, Helene, Isaac, Joyce, Keith, Leslie, Michael, Nadine, Oscar, Patty, Rafael, Sandy, Tony, Valerie, William

2001 Allison, Barry, Chantal, Dean, Erin, Felix, Gabrielle, Humberto, Iris, Jerry, Karen, Lorenzo, Michelle, Noel, Olga, Pablo, Rebekah, Sebastien, Tanya, Van, Wendy

2002 Arthur, Bertha, Cristobal, Dolly, Edouard, Fay, Gustav, Hanna, Isidore, Josephine, Kyle, Lili, Marco, Nana, Omar, Paloma, Rene, Sally, Teddy, Vicky, Wilfred

2003 Ana, Bill, Claudette, Danny, Erika, Fabian, Grace, Henri, Isabel, Juan, Kate, Larry, Mindy, Nicholas, Odette, Peter, Rose, Sam, Teresa, Victor, Wanda

2004 Alex, Bonnie, Charley, Danielle, Earl, Frances, Georges, Hermine, Ivan, Jeanne, Karl, Lisa, Mitch, Nicole, Otto, Paula, Richard, Shary, Tomas, Virginie, Walter

2005 Arlene, Bret, Cindy, Dennis, Emily, Floyd, Gert, Harvey, Irene, Jose, Katrina, Lenny, Maria, Nate, Ophelia, Philippe, Rita, Stan, Tammy, Vince, Wilma

Name _____   Date _____

Disaster Lab: Pressure Drop

PART ONE: AIR POWER

The eye of a hurricane is a calm, low-pressure column of air surrounded by a violent storm. Air from the raging storm sinks into the calm, low-pressure eye, causing it to be cloud-free.

This experiment demonstrates a pressure drop like that found in the eye of a hurricane.

What You'll Need
◈ a glass bottle
◈ a large bowl
◈ water
◈ a small balloon

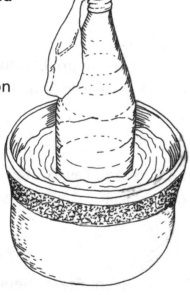

STEP ONE: Fill the bottle with hot water and the bowl with cold water. Let them sit for a minute or two.

STEP TWO: Empty the bottle.

STEP THREE: Stretch the balloon over the mouth of the bottle. Then plunge the bottle in the cold water.

STEP FOUR: As you place the warm bottle in the cold water, the warm air in the bottle cools and contracts. How does this affect the air pressure? How does the difference in air pressure affect the balloon?

PART TWO: MAKE A BAROMETER

Meteorologists use a tool called a barometer to measure air pressure. You can make your own simple barometer.

What You'll Need
◈ a glass or jar
◈ clear plastic wrap
◈ straw from a broom
◈ index card
◈ rubber band
◈ tape

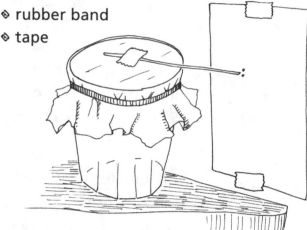

STEP ONE: Place the glass in warm water, then remove it.

STEP TWO: Tightly seal the mouth of the glass with plastic wrap. (Use the rubber band to hold it in place.) Carefully tape the straw to the plastic wrap so that most of the straw hangs over the edge of the glass.

STEP THREE: Tape the index card to the wall at the same height as the glass. Place the glass so that the end of the straw is almost touching the card. Mark the position of the straw on the card.

STEP FOUR: Mark the straw's position every day for five days. Does it move? What is the correlation between the weather and the position of the straw?